CROMWELL

Brendan Kennelly (1936-2021) was born in Ballylongford, Co. Kerry, and was Professor of Modern Literature at Trinity College, Dublin from 1973 until his retirement in 2005. He published more than 30 books of poetry, including *Familiar Strangers: New & Selected Poems 1960-2004* (2004), which includes the whole of his book-length poem *The Man Made of Rain* (1998). He is best-known for two controversial poetry books, *Cromwell*, published in Ireland in 1983 and in Britain by Bloodaxe in 1987, and his epic poem *The Book of Judas* (1991), which topped the Irish bestsellers list: a shorter version was published by Bloodaxe in 2002 as *The Little Book of Judas*. His third epic, *Poetry My Arse* (1995), did much to outdo these in notoriety. All these remain available separately from Bloodaxe, along with his more recent titles: *Glimpses* (2001), *Martial Art* (2003), *Now* (2006), *Reservoir Voices* (2009), *The Essential Brendan Kennelly: Selected Poems*, edited by Terence Brown and Michael Longley, with audio CD (2011), and *Guff* (2013).

His drama titles include *When Then Is Now* (2006), a trilogy of his modern versions of three Greek tragedies (all previously published by Bloodaxe): Sophocles' *Antigone* and Euripides' *Medea* and *The Trojan Women*. His *Antigone* and *The Trojan Women* were both first performed at the Peacock Theatre, Dublin, in 1986 and 1993 respectively; *Medea* premièred in the Dublin Theatre Festival in 1988, toured in England in 1989 and was broadcast by BBC Radio 3. His other plays include Lorca's *Blood Wedding* (Northern Stage, Newcastle & Bloodaxe, 1996).

His translations of Irish poetry are available in *Love of Ireland: Poems from the Irish* (Mercier Press, 1989). He has edited several anthologies, including *The Penguin Book of Irish Verse* (1970/1981), *Ireland's Women: Writings Past and Present*, with Katie Donovan and A. Norman Jeffares (Gill & Macmillan, 1994), and *Dublines*, with Katie Donovan (Bloodaxe Books, 1995), and published two early novels, *The Crooked Cross* (1963) and *The Florentines* (1967).

His *Journey into Joy: Selected Prose*, edited by Åke Persson, was published by Bloodaxe in 1994, along with *Dark Fathers into Light*, a critical anthology on his work edited by Richard Pine. John McDonagh's critical study *Brendan Kennelly: A Host of Ghosts* was published in The Liffey Press's Contemporary Irish Writers series in 2004. His anthology *The Heavy Bear Who Goes with Me* – co-edited with Neil Astley – is due from Bloodaxe in 2022.

CROMWELL

A POEM BY

BRENDAN KENNELLY

BLOODAXE BOOKS

ISBN: 978 1 85224 026 4

This edition first published 1987 by
Bloodaxe Books Ltd,
Eastburn,
South Park,
Hexham,
Northumberland NE46 1BS.

First published 1983 by
Beaver Row Press, Dublin.

www.bloodaxebooks.com
For further information about Bloodaxe titles
please visit our website and join our mailing list
or write to the above address for a catalogue.

Supported using public funding by
**ARTS COUNCIL
ENGLAND**

Digital reprint of the 1987 Bloodaxe Books edition.

For Jim Lydon, my friend –

Note

This poem tries to present the nature and implications of various forms of dream and nightmare, including the nightmare of Irish history. Just as Irish history is inextricably commingled with English history, so is this poem's little hero, M.P.G.M. Buffún Esq., helplessly entangled with Oliver Cromwell as the latter appears and disappears in history, biography, speeches, letters, legend, folklore, fantasy, etc.

The method of the poem is imagistic, not chronological. This seemed to be the most effective way to represent a "relationship" that has produced a singularly tragic mess.

Because of history, an Irish poet, to realise himself, must turn the full attention of his imagination to the English tradition. An English poet committed to the same task need hardly give the smallest thought to things Irish. Every nightmare has its own logic.

History, however, is only a part of this poem. Buffún's nightmare is his own. Hence the fact that he is not a voice; he is many voices.

I wish to acknowledge my debt to Thomas Carlyle's *Oliver Cromwell's Letters And Speeches: With Elucidations* (five volumes, London, 1871); Christopher Hill's *God's Englishman: Oliver Cromwell and the English Revolution* (Pelican, 1970); C.H. Firth's *Cromwell's Army* (Methuen and Co, 1902); Denis Murphy's *Cromwell in Ireland* (M.H. Gill and Son, Dublin, 1883); Merle D'Aubigné's *The Protector* (Oliver and Boyd, Edinburgh, no date on my copy); W.E.H. Lecky's *A History of Ireland in the Eighteenth Century* (London, 1892); Manuscripts of *Depositions of 1641* in the Library of Trinity College, Dublin; Dorothy MacArdle's *Tragedies of Kerry* (Dublin, 1924); and various accounts, mainly in the provincial newspapers and from the conversations of survivors, and of the survivors of survivors, of the Civil War in Ireland, but chiefly in Kerry where it was said to be especially vile, 'a dirty end to a glorious fight'.

Cromwell

Measures

It was just that like certain of my friends I, Buffún, could not endure the emptiness. They took the measures open to them. I invited the butcher into my room and began a dialogue with him, suspecting that he'd follow a strict path of self-justification. Imagine my surprise when, with an honesty unknown to myself (for which God be thanked officially here and now) he spoke of gutted women and ashen cities, hangings and lootings, screaming soldiers and the stratagems of corrupt politicians with a cool sadness, a fluent inevitable pity. But I wasn't going to let that fool me. So, from a mountain of indignant legends, bizarre history, demented rumours and obscene folklore, I accused the butcher not merely of following the most atrocious of humanity's examples (someone was sneezing and shouting 'Mary' outside my room) but also of creating precedents of such immeasurable vileness that his name, when uttered on the lips of the unborn a thousand years hence, would ignite a rage of hate in the hearts of even the most tolerant and gentle. Imagine, I said, to create, deliberately, a name like that for yourself, to toil with such devotion towards your own immortal shame, to elect to be the very source of a tradition of loathing, the butt of jibing, despising millions. (I was really riding the old rhetoric now.)

The butcher calmly replied that the despising millions were simply millions; he was one. One. Yes, I agreed, one who makes Herod look like a benevolent Ballsbridge dad frolicking with his offspring in Herbert Park. I would remind you, returned the butcher, that you invited me here. I am the guest of your imagination, therefore have the grace to hear me out; I am not altogether responsible for the fact that you were reared to hate and fear my name which in modesty I would suggest is not without its own ebullient music. I say further that you too are blind in your way, and now you use me to try to justify that blindness. By your own admission you are empty also. So you invited me to people your emptiness. This I will do without remorse or reward. But kindly remember that you are blind and that I see.

The butcher walked out the door of my emptiness, straight into me.

A Host of Ghosts

Night: the pits are everywhere.
I am slipping into the pit of my own voice,
Snares and traps in plenty there.
If I ponder on shadows in the grass
I will find Oliver, Mum, The Belly, Ed
Spenser down in Cork, the giant, He, a host of ghosts
Who see in the living the apprenticed dead
Merging with insidious mists
Lit here and there by a flashlamp sun
Slaving away like a human mind
To clarify the mist for anyone
Who thinks he'd like to understand
Through nightmare,
      laughter,
        a ridiculous wit,
The symmetry of his particular pit.
If I am nothing, what shall I become?
I here suggest the bobbing sea's débris
Throbbing like Oliver's stimulating drum
Before the export trade in slaves to the Barbados
Inflames my old teacher three hundred years
Later; he stands in the middle of the floor
Raging at rows of shivering youngsters,
Cursing their stupidity and his own anger.
Now he is a ghost as well
Gone to his spot in the symmetry
Of heaven or hell or where you will. You will.
Such happy, tortured ultimates have vanished now
Into the whittling ground
Where dances, for a moment, my nightmare mind.

Oak

On the edge of that firm green land
Looking over black marshes with willows and alders
Oliver Cromwell passed his early years.
Drunken Barnabee, staggering all roads,
Making Latin rhymes through satyr eyes
Sang of an oak-tree
On a hill behind Godmanchester.
Young Cromwell climbed that tree to see
The land he would live and die for.
Branches sustained him, leaves caressed
And blessed him in summer light.
High in the oak, he became a God-listener,
God-speaker, God-lover, God-doer,
God-body, God-mind, God-spirit
And found the wisdom of the Word.
Weakened in manhood, in Windsor Castle,
He climbed to a high room, prayed to his Lord
Who directed his steps
And stated his duty:
Make men of blood account for the blood they'd shed,
For the mischief they'd done to the people of God.

This was the Lord's mercy.

Abysses, pits, chaotic black whirlwinds,
Madness ticks close as madness must
To the mind of a wise man.
But this is not mad, this mind
Is the mother of lightnings and splendours,
This is sane, this, yes, this is most sane.

He

Friday night. He promised us a special treat.
He asked me 'Do you prefer calf or thigh?'
'Calf' I replied. He said 'A moment please.'
He snouted out then and slouched back with a knife.
He mapped thigh and calf in the body of the man
Next to me. It was symmetrically done.
He hi-fied Mozart. This was better than
Anything I'd heard in the village where I was born.
He said to the man arranged at my side
'Sorry about this, I'm afraid it'll hurt you.
But I appreciate your different views.'
He started to cut. The mapped man cried.
I realise I'm somewhat different now
But can't get out of here. Where are my shoes?

Onions

Why this giant? Striding past the Parish Hall
(I'd seen him hoist himself out of the grave,
Spit earth like innocence over the whole
Damned place) he stuck a finger down through the roof
And tasted a slate on the tip of his tongue.
Stepping over the river into Ned's onion-field
He scooped up half-an-acre, started chewing.
Into his face poured a gigantic peace.
If this is the price of peace, I want none
Of it. Ned, Harry and Bat have just arrived
In Bat's Prefect. Like myself, they're all dumb
At the sight of this monstrous resurrection.
Let the bastard chew our onions. We've
Put our heads together now. We'll fix him.

Balloons

Friends beat me up on the way home from school.
Suddenly, a new time happened in me.
It wasn't that I'd come the rough or acted the fool
Too much for them to bear, it was more that they
Needed a victim that June afternoon
When you had to clamp your mouth against the flies
Cancering the air. Since then, I hate June
Because both my hips, under the bruises,
Stopped growing. In the orthopaedic hospital
I'm in the next bed to this Indian
Who can hardly be moved but a bone breaks;
My moon-faced brother looms, his pockets all
Balloons. Weights on my legs, promising man-
hood, suggesting they're the colours of mistakes.

The Ceiling

The way it leaned down on me then I felt
Like a pound note pressed inside a wallet.
I might be used to thin somebody's guilt
Or dropped in a collection to buy bullets
And bombs for those in need of such noises.
Higher up, swallows are making brief homes.
I have never seen mud put to such use.
These builders will fly away from their ruins
And I'll be left, like winter, doubting
The heart of all stabs at architecture,
My own being happily laughable.
If I take it on me to get a house moving
Ceilings will be high as thoughts of disaster,
Unpressing, might as well not be there at all.

The Defender

Under scowling clouds, among bewildering hills
Through which no prisoner could ever escape
To a cleaner bed, more convivial walls,
He established himself as the man in the gap.
He had a range of weapons, sword and gun
Among them, and he used them all
Including his personal vision of the sling-stone
Which his most fanged attackers found hard to swallow.
We had all forgotten the art of
Defence till we saw this black-eyed knacker in
Action through seasons of sun, rain, ice and mud.
Hatred he laughed at, considered offers of love,
Was not averse to the odd feast of meats and wine
And for fun, danced in available blood.

Decisions

This vigilant old Hit is barring me
From joining those I take to be my friends
Having the crack in the midnight Buttery.
He is standing between me and certain sounds
I like. There are nuts who'd assert,
I suppose, that this get has a kind face.
Now that I look at it, I won't hurt
Him. Unless, of course, he continues as he is.
He is guffing about remembering me
From a summer evening six years ago.
Christ! He counts the years! What age was I then?
He's deciding whether to hit me now.
If he does, I'll let him do it. Take blow
Upon blow. Then, once, I'll rock this old man.

A Contribution

'Matters are working for us throughout the world.
There's excellent news from Montague at sea
Turning a Spanish fleet to ashes.
The recent earthquake at Lima
Has helped also. Open your eyes and ears,
Gentlemen, picture thirty-eight wagonloads of silver
Jingling in victory up from Portsmouth
Across London pavements to the Tower
To be coined into English money there.
A glittering river of wealth pours out
From a place of heartbreak and destitution
Because fire and ice are our allies now.
God's Hand is visible in war
When He permits even Antichrist to make a contribution.'

Thanksgiving

Miles Sindercomb tried to murder Cromwell,
Failed. At the Thanksgiving Feast, Oliver said:

'I speak to the best people in the world,
A people who are the apple of God's eye,
A people who will never die,
Not few, but many, a people of the blessing of God,
A people under his protection, close to His Name,
A people to whose homes He is ever welcome,
A people knowing God, a people fearing God
Through laws and statutes close to the Laws of God,
A good God Whose Hand supports this Nation
Rebuking all who would rebuke this Nation.'

Miles Sindercomb ate poison in his cell
Saying 'This is the last time I shall go to bed.'

He snored heavily a while, quietened, died,
Was buried, with due ignominy, on Tower Hill.

Oliver to His Brother

Loving brother, I am glad to hear of your welfare
And that our children have so much leisure
They can travel far to eat cherries.
This is most excusable in my daughter
Who loves that fruit and whom I bless.
Tell her I expect she writes often to me
And that she be kept in some exercise.
Cherries and exercise go well together.
I have delivered my son up to you.
I hope you counsel him; he will need it;
I choose to believe he believes what you say.
I send my affection to all your family.
Let sons and daughters be serious; the age requires it.
I have things to do, all in my own way.
For example, I take not kindly to rebels.
Today, in Burford Churchyard, Cornet Thompson
Was led to the place of execution.
He asked for prayers, got them, died well.
After him, a Corporal, brought to the same place
Set his back against the wall and died.
A third chose to look death in the face,
Stood straight, showed no fear, chilled into his pride.
Men die their different ways
And girls eat cherries
In the Christblessed fields of England.
Some weep. Some have cause. Let weep who will.
Whole floods of brine are at their beck and call.
I have work to do in Ireland.

According to *The Moderate Intelligencer*

This evening, about five of the clock,
The Lord Protector set out for Ireland
In a coach with six gallant Flanders mares
And a life-guard consisting of eighty men:
Ireton, Scroop, Horton, Lambert,
Abbott, Mercer, Fletcher, Garland,
Bolton, Ewer, Cooke, Hewson,
Jones, Monk, Deane. And others.

May God bring Cromwell safe to Dublin
To propagate the Gospel of Christ
Among the barbarous, bloodthirsty Irish
Whose cursing, swearing, drunken ways
Dishonour God by sea and land.

Visit them, Oliver, like God's right hand.

In Dublin

'Swearing, cursing, fighting, drunkenness,
God's Holy Name dishonoured and blasphemed
To the scandal and grief of all good men,
Obscenity the Devil would be hard put to dream,
Nothing but contempt for the laws of the land
And the known articles of war –
I will change the ways of this reeking town
For the good of the Irish poor:

Let the buff coat, instead of the black gown
Appear in Dublin pulpits; God knows it is
Meritorious to use two swords well.
Silence St Austin and Thomas Aquinas,
Let Protestant honesty come into its own.'

He stabled his horses in St Patrick's Cathedral.

A Friend of the People

'Mine was the first Friend's face Ireland ever saw,
Little as it recognised me' Oliver said.
'I came equipped with God's Fact, God's Law.
What did I find? Not men but hordes
Full of hatred, falsity and noise,
Undrilled, unpaid, driving herds of plundered
Cattle before them for subsistence;
Rushing down from hillsides, ambuscadoes,
Passes in the mountains, taking shelter in bogs
Where cavalry could not follow them;
Murder, pillage, conflagration, excommunication,
Wide-flowing blood, bluster high as heaven,
Demons, rabid dogs, wolves. I brought all to heel
Yet my reward was sibylline execration.

Glancing now at my bundle of Irish letters
(A form I think I have perfected)
I see a land run by Sanguinary Quacks
Utterly unconscious of their betters.
Do you think this disease could be cured
By sprinkling it with rose-water
Like a gift of perfume to a flowering daughter?
What could I do with individuals
Whose word was worthless as the barking of dogs?
I addressed the black ravening coil
Of blusterers at Drogheda and elsewhere:

"In this hand, the laws of earth and heaven:
In this, my sword. Obey and live. Refuse and die."

They refused. They died. These letters are fire,
The honest chronicle of my desire,
Rough, shaggy as the Numidian lion,
A style like crags, unkempt, pouring, no lie.'

I Was There

I was there the night I was conceived.
O I grant I wasn't a fly on the ceiling
With his back to what was going on beneath,
Lacking any appropriate feeling
For the start of M.P.G.M. Buffún.
I wasn't a flea in the bed, either,
Choking for air in that creative sweat,
So tiny it couldn't even smother
When bodies' thrashing gasped Beget! Beget!

                          I was a cheeky sperm
Rocketing cockily from flesh to flesh
In the iron bed ruling that damp room
With one window, a chair, two closed doors
And sounds like sighs and moans and farts and snores.

Coal-Dust

It was dear Mummy who put the knife in
First. For two years I'd been her football
And sometimes found myself in the coal-bin,
A succulent darkness that even now retains all
Its promise of tin-lidded security.
Not many men know the taste of coal at
Such an early age, but coal-dust was my
Original love. I lived with it
Even when in a fit worse than usual
Mum prodded my belly with the bread-knife
(Stainless Sheffield) an inch below my little button.
Nothing lethal, you understand. After all
These years, it's the scar I like most in life
And have grown to peek at with some affection.

Family Affairs

Behaviour of some creatures towards their young
Engaged me as I suffered the old goat
Singing *Margaret*, his favourite song.
Not for the first time, I found myself out
Tidying up the parish graves on April
The sixth. With martyrs, dates are precise.
With landlords, monuments are understandable.
Norman Sandes had one, all ivy and moss.
I know I got involved with the ivy,
Ripping it off yet not finding a source,
Piling it high amid gravel and stones.
I saw the hare near a headstone, busy
As I was. Investigating the place
I spied him munching offspring to their bones.

The Curse

The first time I heard the curse in sleep
Was now and a thousand years ago
It didn't assume a pig-shape or dog-shape
Nor was it tarred and feathered like a crow
It wasn't an old soldier talking his wounds
Nor a priest going fifteen rounds with the Devil
It wasn't the smell of blood in killing hands
I'd hardly call it foul

It was more like a small patient hiss
The sound a wind might make trying to be born
A kind of pleading
                          the let-me-have-my-way
Of a child who gets a notion in his
Head to go somewhere
                          only to return
With words like 'I'm back now I want to stay.'

26

You Would Have Blessed Me

The curse was once so virulent in me
I proposed a dialogue
Hoping to find some peace between us.
But the curse kept its silence, cunningly.
I devoured streets, mountains, acres of bog,
Thinking my impassioned stride might dislodge it
But it hugged its root, sticky, meticulous,
Deadly as a man who wants to own something.

I will imagine it as something else, I said
To myself and, glutton that I am,
I dreamed the curse into hot white bread.
I am your womb, I said, and bread is your name.
I tasted the bread. Every crumb was sweet.
You would have blessed me had you seen me eat.

Manager, Perhaps?

The first time I met Oliver Cromwell
The poor man was visibly distressed.
'Buffún' says he, 'things are gone to the devil
In England. So I popped over here for a rest.
Say what you will about Ireland, where on
Earth could a harassed statesman find peace like
This in green unperturbed oblivion?
Good Lord! I'm worn out from intrigue and work.
I'd like a little estate down in Kerry,
A spot of salmon-fishing, riding to hounds.
Good Lord! The very thought makes me delighted.
Being a sporting chap, I'd really love to
Get behind one of the best sides in the land.
Manager, perhaps, of Drogheda United?'

Party

I threw a party for Oliver Cromwell
At the Royal Yacht Club in Dunleary.
He was boring the arse off me with all
His talk about that estate down in Kerry
Where he planned to fish the Cashen and Feale
Till the people would breathe his name in awe.
Bored to my bones, I introduced Cromwell
To the giant who was standing in the harbour,
Cooling off. The giant is not at home in crowds.
Today, as ever, he was very peckish.

'Pleased to meet you, Oliver' the giant said,
'It's not easy having one's head in the clouds
And one's belly yearning. What do you suggest?'

'For starters' Cromwell smiled, 'try twenty thousand dead.'

Magic

Oliver Cromwell's first season as
Manager of Drogheda United was not
Impressive. A bit of a calamit-
y, in fact. 'Get rid of Cromwell' howled
The Drogheda fans, 'Send him to Home Farm,
Athlone, St Pats, Bohemians, U.C.D.
The bastard has brought nothing but harm
To our side. Fling him into the sea!'
Oliver was hauled up before the Board
And asked to account for his performance
Or lack of it. Oliver kept his head.
'We'll top the table yet, I give you my word,
Deep winter approaches, keep your patience,
I'll work magic under floodlights' Oliver said.

The Crowd

One moment I was nothing to the crowd
The next so helplessly a part of it
I had lost what I had come to regard
As myself. I was drowning in a river of hate
I was a jockey on a serpent's back
I was a grub half-way down a sparrow's throat
I was the look Judas threw at the tree
I was fingers fit to handle a pound-note
I was a voice and a sickness of voices
I was a hunger-striker wrapped in a Union Jack
In the rain on a slippery roof in the city
I was crying out to be judged I was
The crime I was the hangman the rope
I was a prisoner longing for love and pity.

The Crowd and the Curse

There is enough whiskey to melt enough ice
There is fire in darkness in raised eyes
The crowd concentrates itself
At one with the heartbeat of the winter night
When the crowd moves the night parts before it
The darkness goes down on its knees to plead
For its life in the freezing wet
The crowd locks at the spot where the boy bled
To death shot in the back by a Tan in a lorry
The crowd is fingers chilling the beads
Breath of hundreds an icicle-prayer
The curse sneers up the road from the sea
The crowd splits the night with its need
The curse and the crowd copulate there.

All His Faces

He's here again, he has all his faces,
He is a besnotted waistcoat, a penknife,
A pipe blackened with Bendigo tobacco,
A priest with a match setting fire to love
Which is ashes in no time, rain tramples it,
He is whiskeybreath, he is grinding his teeth
Boasting of the tall women he screwed
After dances, in cars, flats, moonlit fields,
He is insisting how he did it, he points
To a cow, a bull, he shows with his fingers,
He is eating meat, hot juices pour
Down his mouth, he's a man who knows what he wants,
He's a fat doctor explaining on the stairs
What's wrong, he's the bad word at the door.

The Stare

He stared at her. The stare invaded her eyes
Doing a demolition job on her brain
That had housed her delicate privacies
Years out of mind. The stare strutted down
Into her mouth, dipped, played with her tongue,
Licked into some spittle, swallowed it,
Pronounced it good if a little thin, nothing wrong
With that, might improve, the stare settled down to bite
The inside of her lip, the outside of her neck,
Nipples (naturally) and the sweet meat of each breast
Rising like the cost of loving to the play.
The stare knocked at her sanctum, waited, stuck
Its head in, turned into words fluent as lust
Ripping her up OK stare rules OK.

My Grassy Path

Giving the night its due is hard graft in
Daylight when I'm tempted to walk abroad
And admire each visible delusion.
Uplifting. Yet I do not judge, by God.
Rather do I tend, when possible,
To quit the pavements, patient things, and find
A grassy path, a clump of trees, a pool,
And contemplate the beauty of this land.
Solitude is impossible these days.
An old man with a legendary face
Elects me part of his afternoon dream,
Homers me with inherited stories
Including one of murder in this place.
My grassy path winds back to Deering's scream.

Our Place

The murders are increasingly common
In our place which certain of the old songs
Celebrate as a changeless pastoral heaven.
Due, however, to some folk's sense of wrong
Nothing is right nowadays. I must confess
I've become a bit of a callous bastard
Myself. Sipping the latest atrocities
From our one good paper shows how little I care.

Consider, for example, this morning's gem:
Two youths, both about sixteen, and said
To be savagely bored and out of work
Battered an old man to death in his bed.
Making his sister lie in a style of some shame
They pinned her through the neck with a garden-fork.

Journey to the Golden Man

I went to the Golden Man to find out
About love. Mindful of my scars, I had
Guinness and ham sandwiches on the boat
And patted my wallet to make sure he'd be paid
In full. With fifteen hundred others of
My kind, I beheld him in this huge hall.
His skin was love, his breath was flowing love,
His eyes poured love through my newspaper soul.

Back home, I took it out and read it.
Revelation is what I'm after, but damn
Me, even the sports pages were blank.
Icy water intimidates my heart.
Whenever I see the Golden Man, I am.
I'm water now. Must go again, I think.

A Parable of Pimlico

A kind lady of poorish Pimlico,
Lonely, developed the unusual custom
Of feeding a rat that dared to her door.
Bread, mainly. The rat ate every crumb.
The kind lady relaxed into her chair
Feeling, almost, that she had found a friend.
The rat scoffed offerings with rattish care
Darting the odd glance at the lady's hand.
The lady sickened. The rat nipped to her door
And crossed the ready threshold for the bread
She owed him. But hunger owned the place.
Pimlico neighbours didn't visit her.
As she lay weak, weaker, and yet not dead
The rat sniffed at the hospitable face.

Oliver's Power of Reflection

Oliver's fishing was going so well
In Kerry that he decided to make
Two rivers his own, the Cashen and Feale.
A huge notice, printed on Listowel oak,
Proclaimed that trespassers would be prosec-
uted and, if found guilty, fined or jailed
Or worse. A Subversive Organisation took
Exception to this and wrote to old
Oliver saying they'd blow him up, set fire
To his house, kill his cattle, poison his lands.
'The rabble!' rumbled Oliver, 'The foul sods!'
Yet when he reflected on the matter
He replied, 'Comrades! My grounds are your grounds,
My rivers too. Please bring your hounds, your lines and rods.'

Why?

'I love my little estate down in Kerry'
Smiled Cromwell 'Despite the abominable rain
Which is even worse than England, in my
Opinion. Also, as a gentleman,
I don't mind sharing my fishing rights
With the most fanatical member
Of any Subversive Organisation
Even in the choice months from May to September.
What I detest, however, is tinkers knocking
At my door for money, offering to
Castrate piglets, play fiddles, sing songs, and so on.
The plain truth is that I came here looking
For peace. Then why' whimpered Oliver, 'Why
Can't the natives simply leave me alone?'

Exhortation

'For Christ's sake' the giant said 'And not forgetting
My old pal Dionysus who tends
To scare the wits out of his friends
With his fierce carousing and mad drinking,
Is there any chance that you, in a real
Attempt to hammer sense out of the night
When mares and stallions smash your small mind's gate,
Might, for once, try something on an epic scale?

This world bulges with chirping pissers like yourself,
Melodious dwarfs fluting a dwarfing tune
To other dwarfs who turn their backs
On all songs hacked from nightmare.

Shape up, my little bard! Rattle your rocks!
Give us a twist to ring the ruined moon!'

After Sleep

'I'm enjoying myself hugely' the giant said
'For I have found how succulent are trees.
It was like this. I fell asleep in the shade
Deep in a forest, one of those summer days
When the bigger you are the more wretched
You feel. I suppose my snores rattled the land
Thundering through farmers' comfortable blood,
Driving overworked wives around the bend.

As is my wont, or lot, I then woke up,
Peckish. Could have guzzled a Curragh of horses
But found nothing. No beasts. No wild fruits.
In despair, I broke an oak, tried a chip,
Relished it, scoffed the lot, replenished my forces.
I think I'll chew forests down to their roots.'

Instruments

I saw the hand distilling a desert out
Of itself all of a May morning.
Then, patiently, it began to create
A cathedral in the desert, building
Day and night, scorning the thought of rest.
It made people out of the sand,
Guided them into the cathedral, blessed
Them as they gazed speechlessly at their surround-
ings. Here and there, a man, a woman began
To pray. The hand moved to a green country
Near the desert and with its forefinger
Made a black crack in the earth. Very soon
The desert split open, a huge wound. The
Cathedral collapsed into the hole. People died there.
No one was recovered, the time was too deep.
Centuries passed, or seemed to, the wound healed
But not before pain-language was born. Up
From the hole it crept, shy, into the world.
The hand, watching, ordered it to go among
This peaceful tribe who had to fight
To stay alive. The language became song,
The hand said, I will play for you tonight.
So, choosing some of the best preserved bones
From that familiar hole in the desert
The hand made instruments for all to see
And played them with love. People are not stones.
The music touched and opened every heart.
No music touches it, we all agree.

The Matter of Ointment

The day the snake slithered into our village
There was a scatter among the citizens
Who'd never forgotten the snake's atrocious
Reputation in the literature of the ages.

There was this girl with sweetly-chiselled lips
Who walked up to the reptile and murmured
'It has long been my ambition to dance for you
And to salve your body with my home-made ointment.'

'That suits me' smiled the snake 'I'll hiss for you
That we may find a rhythm congenial to us both.'
He hissed. She danced. It was a harmonious moment.

The girl, as promised, salved the snake's body.
He wriggled in ecstasy and hissed 'The truth
Is I'm vain as most men, in the matter of ointment.'

Some Family Instructions

I could have sworn it was the mighty whine
Of an elephant I heard as I turned
The bleeding steak on its back. I do not like mine
Bloody, I do not like it burned,
I'm a maniac for medium. I
Expected elephants when I looked round
The corner. Imagine my surprise when I saw
A senior alligator instructing his family how
To eat. 'First' he jawed, 'Let four of you
Squat on this impressive elephant
So that he can't stir. Then let the others
Eat the elephant alive. When they've had
Enough, let eaters switch places with sitters.
Co-operate. You are sisters and brothers.'

The Arranging Hand

The hand reached down out of the sky,
Hovered above the fields, the trees, the road.
Poised above a crossing, it said to me,
'I shall arrange this scene before the blood
Spilled, before the accident, I mean.
Here is the Cortina, nosing from the side.
Notice the driver, mooning at the wheel.
And here is the truck, roaring as it should

Into the Cortina's body.' The hand did
What the hand said. I saw it all before
It happened. I saw it afterwards too.

The Cortina, folded, was sweating blood.
The truck-driver backed from his cab to stare
At the other driver who had nothing to say.

Transfigurations

The hand turned itself into a meat-crusher
(It could be used for vegetables too)
And beckoning to B. Gorman, waiter,
Lopped off the fingers of his right hand in a
Jiffy, swallowed them as a priest would wine,
Initiated a crushing process within
Itself, bones powdering, flesh melting, then
Oozed a dark sludge. This was part of man
Transfigured into a sustaining drink.
B. Gorman himself was the first to sip
Himself. Himself had a quick effect on him.
'I am water' he said, 'Watch me as I sink.
I am blood in this chalice at my lip.
I am a hunter, and my own victim.'

I Can't Say What's Wrong

I see a man bidding for a woman
A woman bidding for a man.
The auctioneer is fat, sweating profit.
Doctor Silver should put him on a diet.

What an arena! Amid tables and chairs
And three thousand books signed Fanny Partridge
I am tempted to prowl and rummage
Till I grab the exact items I'm after.

But no, feeble-minded clod, I resume my stare
At whoever is bidding for whom
In this money-electric auction-room.

Somebody has bought somebody for a song.

They're leaving together. The auctioneer
Sweats a smile. I can't say what's wrong.

Pennies

The dwarf bought a penny whistle
Played a penny song
Dwarf colleagues cheered and praised him
Till his beard grew long

His head got bumpy and bigger
His chest was a hump in front
Of the other hump at his back
He was a famous runt

Travelling to many places
Some far over the sea
He delivered the songs he was paid for

Fingering his whistle to faces
With careful ecstasy

He played what the faces called for.

An Old Murderer's Gift

'Mister Buffún' lisped the old murderer
From under his tattered ancient cape,
Twisted fingers twisting his cloth cap,
'I'm your friend, a thousand-year-old soldier
With fond memories of looting and rape,
Gutting of cities, towns and villages
And, best of all, terror on the faces
Of men, women and children with no escape.
Yes, I throttled words in many a throat
And saw the blood boiling in their eyes
When they stared into the face of silence.
I've witnessed this for centuries. Not
A pretty sight. But out of it, for you, this
Language I bring, blood-born, for your convenience.'

A Language

I had a language once.
I was at home there.
Someone murdered it
Buried it somewhere.
I use different words now
Without skill, truly as I can.
A man without a language
Is half a man, if he's lucky.

Sometimes the lost words flare from their grave.
Why do I think then of angels,
Seraphim, Cherubim, Thrones, Dominions, Powers?
I gaze amazed at them from far away.
They are starting to dance, they are
Shaping themselves into vengefully beautiful flowers.

That Word

'Never let me hear you mentioning that word!
To you it may suggest legends of rocks and fields
Bluster about illuminated books
Stories of the sea
Conspiring to change your state. It may be for you
A way of experiencing the seasons, learning the ways
Of birds and animals extinct elsewhere. Or it may
Stir the people to question what is obviously
A satisfactory condition. Therefore, I forbid you
To use that word. Banish it from the language
Into that exile where certain words pine and die
Like members of your own family who
Couldn't find work at home and had to slave
So hard in other countries they forgot to ask why.'

What Use?

'What use is that language to a man out of work?
A fat bastard of a teacher rammed it down my throat
For eight years before I could quit
That school where I learned nothing
But Sorrowful, Joyful and Glorious Mysteries
And answers to questions I never understood
And that damned language bringing tears to my eyes
Every time I struggled to say a word.
Can you see me facing a foreman in England
Equipped with my native sounds, asking for a start
To prove I can use my hands
Like any other man from any other land?
That language should have been choked at birth
To stop it wasting my heart and mind.'

Someone, Somewhere

'I do not believe this language is dead.
Not a thousand years of hate could kill it,
Or worse, a thousand years of indifference.
So long as I live my language shall live
Because it is mine, do you hear me, mine,
No, of course you don't hear me, why should you,
You who believe what has always been said,
Let us bury our language, our language is dead.
I have a notion, I have a bike
And I'm going to ride it through the back roads
Of Ireland. Each road, in its turn,
Will twist me to people, my people, whose minds
Will dance to those words buried
In their hearts. Someone, somewhere, will learn.'

A Man of Faith

'Buff' said Oliver, 'Some poor sad prattling priest
May have spoken to you of faith,
Thinking your soul might work towards its best
And understand God's reasons for death.
Your poor sad prattling priest was right, or partly so.
This gutless age sinsickens in disbelief,
Only a man of faith will do, will rise and do
What he must do, be it smooth or rough.
A man of faith is a ready blade
Cutting through the bluster of himself, his time,
Friends, enemies. He lives for what is true
In himself. I am such a man, not more, not less.
Some say my faith is lies, my best deeds crimes.
I believe in God Who believes in what I do.'

Beach Scene

I saw Mum as a child of six playing
On a beach one frolicsome August day.
She was wearing a lemon mini-bikini
And ignored me when I edged her way.
A warm breeze swooned in from the Atlantic,
Bronzed strangers stretched or curled on the sand,
Mum glanced at me. I went up to her quick-
ly and said 'I'm your son, my girl, and
I'd like to introduce myself without
Delay. You're going to spawn me in twenty years.
Let's meet before the coming gets rough.'
Mum looked at me, the old distrust and doubt
Glared into me, piercing my filial tears.
She threw sand at my eyes and hissed 'Piss off!'
If there's one thing I won't do for a six-
Year-old, it's piss off when she orders me.
And yet, because I'm not a man of tricks
Or given to emotional chicanery,
And also since I'm interested in Mum
And her development from nappy-rash
To wholesome couplings with choice lumps of flesh,
I showed no anger but said 'Will you come
Play with me, please, please!'
                              That persuaded her.
'O.K.' she said. 'What shall we play?' I asked.
'Computers' she replied 'And robbing banks.
Come on, let's see your knife, your new revolver,
Your balaclava helmet. O sad old man,
Where are your bombs, your dynamite, your tanks?'

5½ lbs

I saw myself seeing myself seeing her there
Giving birth to me that oozy night.
5½ lbs. I was, if the scales were right.
(They rarely are.)
Look at me now, tubful of meditative guts.
Meditative? I wouldn't know a thought if I saw one
Playing pitch-and-toss with the urchins and brats
I was reared with. Now I'm a man.
A man? As a slightly promoted beast
I question that term, I, a temple of the Holy Ghost,
That happy impulse, elusive spirit of cosmic good-will.
I close my eyes again and again I'm dreaming
Of a sappy man and a woman screaming.
I see myself seeing myself seeing her still.
Who am I kidding? So I think I see her then?
She looks at me now, sees me, reads me
Like a postcard from Brighton or Ballybunion.
I have sent her greetings, wished she was here
Wherever it is, there's a smell of tar,
Crouched men are making a road,
It's bound to lead somewhere, she sees me,
She smiles, cries, she's already receding,
Is there anyone who isn't fading?
She fades into clarity, a tide revealing rocks,
Gouged shells, small pools, reminders of the sea
That has wandered away like a prodigal son
To find himself among go-slows and lightning strikes
And bids for power and rumours of his own excesses
Which seem, in retrospect, little or nothing to have done.

Oliver's Mantra

'I really like my name' Oliver said
'When I was under pressure in England
Trying to knock sense into stupid heads
That couldn't even begin to understand
My simple yet sublime designs for my
Country, I often popped into a room,
Alone, and there closing my eyes in a
Deliberate act of contemplation,
I invoked my mantra. It was, of course,
My name, the one source of comfort to me.
Oliver Cromwell! Oliver Cromwell!

Oliver Cromwell!

        I grew strong as a horse,
Sly as a fox, wise as I am now. I
Heard my name throb in my soul. Beautiful!'

Oliver's Vision

'Names that are loved are of men who've done good.
Sometimes, sitting in the dark, meditating
On the knotted style of decent God
Whose will I never tire of executing
Despite the stratagems of hostile men,
I believe I see a child, a boy, as yet
Unborn, English, Irish, finding he's alone
In this world of normal clods and humanbrute
Innuendo: he looks about him. What
Shall he do? How answer riddling voices?
In this coarse world, how touch something fine?
What images inspire? What name is right?

When the mind finds the name, the heart rejoices.
The boy discovers it one day. It's mine.'

Stones and Pebbles and the Language of Heaven

'I must confess, Buffún' honestied Oliver
'Your native language strikes me as barbarous,
Rude in the mouth, agony on the ear,
Your very name's ridiculous
Suggesting some aboriginal fool
Astray where he should be most at home.
Stones and pebbles cram every native mouth, Buffún.

Quit this confusion.

If the people of England are the people of God
Then England's language is the language of heaven
Which every Christian gentleman should use.
Immerse yourself in that felicitous tongue,
Absorb its magic through proper attention,
Utter yourself, universalise your views.'

Ghouls

'What? Me, a humorist? Never! Not me!'
Cried Oliver, 'I'll leave that to you, Buffún.
Yet, looking at the ghouls of history,
I see how laughter might engulf a man.
Massacres, my best men tell me, are fun,
The only fun a common soldier has
After six months or a year in the waste.
A soldier has a feeling for his gun
And likes to use it. I recall a town
Where my army went on the rampage.
I heard them laughing. They had a ball,
Splitting the women. Well, Buffún, they were men.
I sat astride a stallion, a little off-stage.
He was a noble brute, throbbing. We saw it all.'

The Words Are Warm

Rumours of love keep drifting back to me
As if, in another country, I'd known
Someone who loved me but scarpered in a hurry.
There are times I feel like pursuing that man
Or woman but this would probably take
Ages so that I'd be a greyhaired crank
Scouring valley and mountain, river and lake
For love that came and vanished like a wink.

OK, so I'd find it or something like
It in the end or somewhere near the end.
I imagine a lowish house with dripping eaves.
'Who are you?' I ask the figure at the fire.
'I think' – the words are warm – 'I'm a friend
And I'm here to love you before I leave.'

I Saw a Beautiful Man

I saw a beautiful man and he
Was uglier than me or you
He was a beautiful man because I
Had the eyes to see him true
And then my eyes went blind a while
I saw a mean man standing there
With lips like snakes, his eyes snake's eyes,
Snakespittle dribbling from his hair.

Then I slept, sleep changed my eyes,
My eyes were cleaned, I saw again
The beautiful man
Standing there, happy and wise
For those who had eyes to see.
What strikes his eyes when he looks through me?

To Such as Me

The Golden Man went on a lecture tour of
European Capitals. His subject,
Which had been widely paperbacked, was Love.
Out to influence every church and sect

He read himself with intellectual lust,
Determined to put all men in the picture.
Good of him to start with me. One night, he crossed
The Irish Sea and gave me a lecture.

It is not likely I'll receive again
Such insights into Love. I heard them too
In the attentive air of my own home.

I munch the wisdom of the Golden Man
While he reveals the meaning of true
Love to such as me in Berlin, Paris, Rome.

Trout

He's here again. We're in church. He's a bishop.
He has a long pink forefinger which he
Keeps jabbing too close to my right eye.
He wears crowblack clothes. I'm all dickied up

In a new suit myself. Confirmation Day.
He opens his mouth, I can see his lips,
His teeth off-brown, his tongue placid as a
Trout resting on a hot day in the shade

Of an overhanging bank. His face is
So near mine I could swim through his eyes.
'What's peace?' he asks.

　　　　　'The ha-ha-harmony of the sus-sus-soul
With Gug-Gug-God' I reply. 'Beautiful' smiles the trout,
'You are now a soldier of Christ. Go out,
Fight for him. God bless you, my son. That is all.'

Hovering

The wolf is here all night, won't nose away
Or lope out into this poor light
Where I lie. Some other buff might
Call this skulking but I, being here, do not.
I call it hovering. This wolf knows about edges,
He's not too deep in the dark, but deep
Enough to make himself present
And play with, being absent, the toy of my sleep.

Just beyond is where he hovers, just beyond.

I strain eyes, ears, but he defines me
As though I'll never break past the range of flame
And must wait here, full of him, gorged with wolf
While he makes me doubt all I am and am
Not, sieged by the milling syllables of my name.

Mum's Tongue

Mum's tongue snaked after me
I ran three different roads at once
I hid in cottages in the basements
Of Youth Hostels Anglo-Irish mansions
But Mum's tongue snaked after me
Cold and long and dripping poison
Screaming kiss me kiss me kiss me
I covered myself with leaves in a cabbage-garden
I went to Midnight Mass
I offered my heart to The Sacrifice
I became a customer at an Allied Irish Bank
I was a jarvey up and down Moll's Gap
But Mum's tongue snaked after me till I
Turned and drank sweet Jesus how I drank

A Sound of Breaking

It was forgiveness in the voice I heard
God alone knows how many years after,
Drifting down that rainy street
Out into the destroyed river
Dead as money harnessing us all.

I see him tall and smiling, her in a blue dress.
It is after midnight, a black, resonant pool.
Already in the air the taste of ashes
Is growing powerful and sour,
There is a sound of breaking
Like a bone in a game but nobody is sure.
I have to get away from here
Out of reach of crying, beyond range of wrecking
A moment that cannot, given such bondings, endure.

Dedication

'Most fair and virtuous lady' wrote Ed,
'I am happy to make known to you
The humble affection I have always professed
And bear to that House from which your true
Heart springs. Therefore I present to you these
Idle labours composed in the raw conceit
Of my youth. Simple is the device,
The composition mean. Yet I dare to set
Them at your feet, hoping they may catch your eye
And that I may receive your noble favour.
One moment's joy to you justifies the work
Of all my days. Your Honour's humbly ever,
                              Edmund Spenser.'

            Ed sealed the poem and sighed,
'Anything to escape from fucking Cork!'

Her Cries

This young lady of milky countenance
Who in middle-age will grow a dark moustache
Become an addict of Russian folk-dance
And choose, every second Monday night, to wash
Her delighted body in tepid water,
Is crying in front of the Public Library,
Crying out of an undisguisable fear,
'Please, sir, please don't ask me
To get in that damned car with him.'
I approach this man whose brute eyes
Emphasise his Adonis form.
I say what the milky lady said.
The air bears all her fearing cries.
Through his eyes the demons thrive and swarm.

The Griefs

One by one, the griefs slipped out of me
And went off to Ballybunion
For a weekend in a pub by the sea.
Here are the shape-changers, droppers of identity,
Masters of becoming whatever they will.
The air itself collaborates with them.
One became the shuffle of a sensible
Civil Servant who disliked his own name
Because it belonged to his father;
One set up house with the scruples
Of a man determined not to be;
Another went into a girl opening her
Legs in a hole among the sandhills;
One came back to me.

History

'I have this learned friend at Oxford'
Chimed Oliver. 'He teaches history
To young gentlemen who should know the state
Of things because one day, like it or not, they
Must grow up to do what they must do.
My friend is a fine athlete. He keeps fit.
Mens sana in corpore sano is his motto.
He likes a jar as well. I confess that
Now and then the pair of us get blotto.

But when he talks to me of history
I have to smile. This tends to madden him.
"Cromwell, your smiling has always attacked
My views of history. What *is* history then?
You tell me."
                    I let him wait for my reply.

"History is when I decide to act." '

In Oliver's Army

No man shall depart a mile out of the Army, upon pain of death
No man shall draw his sword without order, upon pain of death
No man shall hurt a man bringing food, upon pain of death
A sentinel asleep or drunk or forsaking his place shall die without mercy
No man shall give a false Alarum, upon pain of death
He that makes known the Watchword without Order shall die for it
If a Pike-man throw away his pike, he shall die for that
No man shall abandon his colours, upon pain of death
None shall kill an Enemy who yields and throws down his Armes
Rape, Ravishments, Unnatural Abuses shall meet with death
Let God be served, Religion be frequented
Let sellers of meat avoid the unsound, the unwholesome
Let Heaven be praised with sermon and prayer
Let all faults be punished by the Laws of War.

The Enemy

'Divers of The Enemy retreated into Mill-Mount'
Chronicled Oliver, 'A strong place, difficult of access,
Exceedingly high, having a good graft,
Firmly palisadoed. I captured the place
And ordered my men to put the Governor,
Sir Arthur Aston, and considerable officers
To the sword. Indeed, being in the heat
Of action, I forbade my men to spare
Any of The Enemy in the town.
A hundred such sought refuge in St Peter's
Church-steeple. I offered mercy to each in turn.
They refused. I ordered the steeple to be burned down.
In the midst of the flames, one of the creatures
Shrieked: "God damn me, God confound me; I burn, I burn."'

That Leg

Sir Arthur Aston had a wooden leg.
He hid his gold in it, the world said.
A fierce dispute arose among the soldiers
Concerning that wealthy lump of wood.
They seized the prize when good Sir Arthur fell.
Examining it, they found it had no gold,
That leg was but pure wood.
The soldiers bashed his brains with it for old
Time's sake, then hacked his body to pieces.
Was a dead man ever so roundly cursed
By honest soldiers at their work of blood?
But wait! Tom Fowler picks Sir Arthur's girdle
And leaps with joy to find therein
Two hundred golden pieces, quilted.

A Bad Time

Having butchered everyone in the church
The soldiers explore the vaults underneath
Where the choicest ladies are hidden
Hoping to cheat the general death.
One of these, a most handsome virgin,
Kneels down to Thomas à Wood, with prayers
And tears, that he may spare her life.
Sudden pity; he takes her in his arms
Out of the church, intending her escape.
A soldier sees this and pikes her through.
À Wood, seeing her gasping, takes her money
And jewels, flings her down over the works.
Massacre flows for five days in succession.
A bad time for virgins, local people say.

The Soldiers

The soldiers cut the head, hands and feet off the crucifix
They load themselves with the citizens' goods
They excavate the crypts, break open the marble
Tombs in hope of plunder, they fill the church
With corpses, they dress in the precious vestments,
They invite a few trampled souls to Mass
They dash the holy images against the walls
And bear a headless statue of the Virgin in procession.
'How now, Mary of Ireland, how now? Eat some peas'
A soldier calls but a stone falls on his head.
He is not pretty.
Blood continues to run in the streets
Warmer now than ever it ran in human veins
Because the soldiers have set fire to the city.

The Lugworms Know

'There's nothing as funny as nightmares,
Especially afterwards' Oliver said.
'Mine are lugworms swelling at my door,
Sandy, ever-fattening bodies, small heads
Fanged like traitors' minds at court or where
You will. Sometimes they tunnel through my blood,
Stick their snouts up through the roots of my hair.
Next day, I hear you think, I don't feel good.
How wrong you are, Buffún, old chap!
I may be a little morbid at breakfast
But about noon, with my sandshovel, I go
To the beach and dig some lugworms up.
I peer at them for hours and then I laugh
And laugh. Why? Can't say. The lugworms know.'

Severest Friend

'The last intention in my heart was to harm you'
Oliver said,
'I came here knowing I had Surgery to do
That you and yours be more alive than dead,
Saved from your self-wasting ways.
I am your severest friend, and your best.
I speak and act like the honest
Man I am, beyond the world's blame and praise.

Write down this in the blank page of your mind.
"Cromwell is my friend as England is my friend,
And will be, if I obey, to the end of time."

Ponder these simple, deep, unending words.
Do as each word bids.
Do not, you will be punished for your crime.'

Oliver Writes to the Speaker of
the Parliament of England

'Sir, our hardships are not a few.
If moneys be not supplied
I cannot finish this good work.
I would not dare say this if I did
Not reckon it my duty so to do.

Our horse have not had one month's pay of five.
We strain what we can that the Foot be paid.
On almost nothing, I keep a whole army alive.

There are many towns to be reduced.
This must needs swallow up our Foot.
How shall I drive them? The whip? The rod?
This country has taught me the nature of waste,
I would be honest; waste me not,
I need moneys to fulfil the will of God.
His voice is clamouring for action, now.
If God be for us, who can be against us?
Who can rebel against the Lord and prosper?
Who can resist His will and not be lost?

May the Lord keep us in His love forever.

Sir, I humbly wish to know your will
To follow your commands with all alacrity
Rejoicing in the work my superiors tell
Me to do. This I acknowledge you to be,
Fearing only in obeying you, to disobey you.
I desire your prayers; you are often in mine.
I pray to be obedient, cheerful too
That I gather what the Lord scatters in my way.
More moneys, I shall perfect your noble plan.
Praise God it is your work I do,
Immortal dignity for mortal man.'

Oliver to His Army

'I judge it to be displeasing to God
That any Officer or Soldier of this Army
Marry with some Papist slut. Any
Officer who marries any such shall be
Judged incapable of command or trust
In this Army; any Soldier that marries any such,
If he be horseman, shall be dismounted
To serve only in foot service (if at all);
A footman so married shall be cashiered
From service and serve only as a Pioneer.
None such will get preferment in the future.
How should he? These sinful contracts
Can do no more than spark God's anger,
Bring his displeasure on us, some way or other.'

Tongues

Well, as the soldier-poet observed, there were
Few soldiers who
                        'rather than turn
From English principles, would sooner burn;
And rather than marry an Irish wife
Would bachelors remain for term of life'.

Good men trained to kill will turn to love
When they grow tired of killing
And word cavorts abroad that local
Girls are willing.

But worst of all the men who tamed
Drogheda and Wexford and Dublin town
Wedded these wenches, barbarous and young.
Their children and their children's children grew
To scorn the English, love the Irish tongue.

Work and Play

Killing children is not pleasant, even in the worst of times.
Oliver's boys
Approached the task with Herodean vigour
And discipline to put us all to shame.
With no tea-break, overtime or danger-money,
With small thought for their own safety
Oliver's boys
Spent themselves in the little killings
And never complained
Even when ordered to pile the small
Bodies into hastily-dug pits.
They filled in the pits with fresh clay.
There should be a playground for small ghosts
Somewhere. I think so. What have you to say?

Why?

Drink, boy, they said. Why? he asked.
Your father grabbed our land, they said.
He started to drink the whiskey from the cask.
Drink more, they said, let's makebelieve it's blood.

Take your clothes off, boy, they said.
Why? he mumbled.
Your father grabbed our land, they said.
They whipped him naked along the road.

They hanged him once, then yanked him down.
They hanged him twice and hauled him down.
Third time they let him swing.

Nits will make lice, they said.
Drunken nits look better off the ground
And father-lice may tumble to what's wrong.

The Dose

'Strip her.
Whip her through the town.
Fling her into the river
From the bridge in Portadown.
Take her sister then
To a big important Protestant house.
Strip her, strip the owner, strip his working men and women.
Turn them all to ashes.

Retire to a nearby hillside,
Have a drink, relax, enjoy the screams, the flames.
The purged night,
Repeat the dose all through the province.
It is, you'll agree, satisfying work.
Don't delay, brothers. Get on with it.'

Story

I believe my eyes, I'm in a distant country,
I have lost my brothers and sisters
I am hiding, I must tell my story:
Last evening, soldiers drove the catechists
Out of the forest into the village,
I saw my brother, fingernails and toenails gone,
Black stumps for feet, all his friends the same,
The soldiers covered them with petrol
Set fire to them
I saw my brother become flame
Flame become cries
I watched
I have a story for someone
I can tell it with my eyes.

Clean

'You know what these Irish bitches are like.
When they're not holy, they're cannibals
Out to munch a man's prick and balls
As an afternoon snack.
There was this mountainous cow of a creature
Who liked to kill and devour others
In a manner not uncommon among Irish mothers.
I decided to hang her.
She was no graceless that not once
Did she cry or call upon God to forgive her
But dangled in silence, gross and obscene.
Afterwards, I went to her house
And found the bones of three of my troopers
Picked clean.'

Birthmark

'A gentleman of the troop of the Boyles
Dropped in and cut griskins or collops
Of William Stewart alive;
Stuffing fire-coals into his mouth
He ripped up his belly
Wrapped his entrails about his neck.
It was grisly to see
And yet in all this chopping of Mr Stewart
I was struck by one quiet detail
As people sometimes are
In the midst of howling scenes;
A birthmark on his left breast
Shaped like a broken star.'

'Do Good'

'I suppose this Protestant wretch
Thought he'd be safe in his grave
Stretched neatly beside his bitch
As was, indeed, his death-wish.
Granted, of course. We dug him up,
Mammocked his coffin, threw his carcass over the wall
Of the graveyard. There where he fell
I stuck on his head his heretic's cap.

The land of Kildare will never be sanctified
Till the last heretic's bones
Are plucked from the clay and destroyed.
They must not escape just because they are dead.
Death brings no pardon to guilty skeletons.
Know this. Then go and do good.'

Rebecca Hill

Half-hanging is the rage in Kildare
It is the rebels' will
So died Jonas Wheeler William Dandy James Benn
Rebecca Hill

Rebecca Hill was fifteen years
Half-hanged then taken down
As comely a girl as ever walked
Through Kildare Town

Taken half-hanged from an oak-tree
She seemed to recover her wits
The rebels saw her flutter alive
Then buried her quick

Leaves of the oak-tree still
Flutter like Rebecca Hill.

Siege

'God damn me, God sink me, God make me a rat
If ever I raise my siege of this town
Till I starve all the heretics out.
I swear by my Saviour that I, as an Irishman,
Will never leave these walls
Till I have eaten Sir Henry Tichbourne's heart
And every one of his soldiers
Has sucked the marrow of Protestant bone.
You dare to ask me, What shall I do
With the English in this garrison?
O I have a part for them, a pretty part:
I'll blow them up
And make gunpowder out of them.
Worse than dogs, they are no Christians.
Protestants must be christened again at Mass
Before they are Christians. They are not human,
They are beasts, if they persist as beasts
I'll answer by hanging, drowning in rivers,
Ditches and holes, I'll answer by burning,
The sword, stripping, famishing, starving
And other ways. I give them my warning
Now: to kill the English as they are
Is no more pity than killing dogs.
How else treat the enemies of God?
The brains of cows dead of diseases
Boiled with nettles and weeds – let that be their fare
Till they change from beasts and turn to the good.'

She

She hears a landlord speak of the advantages of death
She goes through flames to save herself
She has a son murdered
She eats rawhides drinks puddles
She tries two churches
She cocks her piece and shoots a lord
She becomes a widow
She witnesses the burning of Lurgan
She sees Ruth Lynn hanged by the hair of the head
Anne Butler's brains scattered on stones
Toole McCann cut in pieces
Jane Hazleton die
Giles Whitehead burn
She does not ask why.

A Holy War

'We suffered the little children to be cut out of women
"Their bellys were rippitt upp"
This was a holy war, a just rebellion
And little lords in the womb must not escape
Their due. Certain women not great with child
Were stripped and made to dig a hole
Big enough to contain them all.
We buried these women alive
And covered them with rubbish, earth and stones.
Some who were not properly smothered
Yet could not rise
(They tried hard) got for their pains
Our pykes in their breasts. People heard
(Or said they heard) the ground make women's cries.'

The Soldiers' Song

The devil sweep whoever led us
Out of the land of sunny Spain
Where we drank and ate like honoured heroes
Tended by soft women

To this beggarly curse-o'-God
Country where nothing thrives
But hunger and cold and heart's hatred
Blackening people's lives

In that other land we lived
Bravely and well
Here we do nothing but rehearse
Eternal hell

Lead us from this renegade place
To fight true enemies face to face.

Some People

Elizabeth Birch had a white neck
They roped it
George Butterwick of the strong body
Looked awkward naked
Sylvanus Bullock liked riding the highway
Died stripped in a ditch
John Dawling a brave swimmer
Drowned thrown off Belturbet bridge
George Netter a providing father
Perished with his five starved children
Philip Lockington a big farmer
Was flogged to an idiot beggar
Oliver Pinder offered shelter to people of the road
His house was pulled down over his head

May the Lord have mercy on the dead.

Oliver Speaks to His Countrymen

I have no rhetoric, no wit, no words.
The Dispensations of God upon me
Require I speak not words, but Things.

I speak of the Being of England,
Of the endeavour and design of its common Enemies
Whether abroad or at home
In London or in Rome.
I will now specificate our Enemies.

Our great Enemy is the Spaniard.
The hatred in the Spaniard is the hatred of God.
Led on by superstition from the See of Rome
The Spaniard will never come to good.
Have no trade with him; with him your only trade
Is duel to the death. Consider
The Spaniard's invasion of Ireland,
His designs of the same kind upon England,
Public designs, private designs, all manner of designs
To accomplish this great and general end.
If you do not know your Enemy, you cannot know your Friend.
Know this: we'll suffer more from peace with Spain
Than from Spain's intense hostility.
When Philip the Second married Queen Mary
And since that time, through Spanish instigation,
Twenty thousand Protestants were murdered in Ireland,
I think it my duty to win by the sword
What is not to be had otherwise.
The sharpest sword is the sharpest word.
This is the spirit of Englishmen.
If so, it is the spirit of men who have higher spirits,
Men who are Englishmen and more,
Believers in God's Gospel –
Clumsily said, but not clumsily meant.
England is Protestant
And will be to the end.
(Know your Enemy: know your Friend.)

Our danger from the Common Enemy abroad,

The Devil apeing the Face of God,
Is headed by the Pope,
Leader of the anti-Christian Interest.
He has an interest in your bowels; he has so.
This is the danger you must know.

At home, there is danger from Priests and Jesuits,
Papists and Cavaliers.
Dark, spectral Jesuits, the Spaniard,
Levellers and discontented persons
Make one black anti-Christian mass
To overwhelm us all. I am an outcast from eloquence,
I have poor words, yet speak my Nation's will.
When my Nation is threatened, I grieve
And do my duty, though men may not believe.
Therefore, I will not cease to say
England cannot be safe
Until Malignants be swept away.
This Pope has a certain zeal for his religion,
A man of contrivance, wisdom, and policy.
He wishes to unite all popish Interests
In the Christian world, against this Nation above any,
Against all the Protestant Interest in the world.
I will not shake the hand of such a man.
Christ and Antichrist had better not
Shake hands; no good will come of it.

I speak plainly. I have no words, no wit.
I love England. I love the very thought of it.

I would lay open the danger
Where in my conscience I know we stand.
If you do not see what is obvious here
We shall sink, our house will fall about our ears.
I tell you plainly what is dangerous.

I see what threatens us.
I know what is.
Sluggish men will not acknowledge this,
Preferring the happiness of lies.
I see what is. I speak what is.
These are things – not words!

Here is a Thing.
An officer was engaged to seize me in my bed
And shoot me dead;
Another, to put gunpowder in my room
And blow me up.
Both these men are gone to their doom
But not I to mine.
I'll wait awhile. There are battles to win.
Herod and Pilate were reconciled
That Christ might die.
Some Fifth-Monarchy men and Commonwealth men
Are reconciled in their dislike of me.
These are unquiet men, a troubled sea
That cannot rest, its waters throw up
Mire and dirt, such men we find
Leading the bloody massacres in Ireland,
Such troubled men I here pronounce to be
Against the Interest of England.

To be English is to be more than English:
It is to be a Christian man
Who knows Jesus Christ:
To be English is to face the hardest test.

To be English is never to quibble about words
Or matters of no moment.
It is to have a conscience and be free
To enjoy that conscience.
To be English is to believe in Christ
In the remission of sins through His blood
In the grace of God,
To know the debt we owe to God
When we enjoy our liberty.

True tolerance is noble,
True intolerance nobler still.

Hate the inessential.

Study books, if you will.
Study your own hearts, if you are able.

66

A man is a mind, the mind is the man.
Otherwise, he's a beast.

If I had the tongue of an Angel
If I were inspired as men of God have been
I could live in you till you would live
To save your nation.
You are the true Protestants of this world.
Do not go blind-eyed into ruin.
If a man scruple the plain truth before him
It is vain to meddle with him.
Leave him alone to shipwreck his soul.
Let him eat the heart of his own will.

My countrymen, who live in my heart,
Have peace among yourselves.
I am in union with you, united
In faith and love with Jesus Christ
And his peculiar Interest.
If that is not true, let me curse myself
And pray God may curse me too!
I know too much of God to fool with Him
Or be bold with Him in these things.
I hope I never shall be bold with Him
Who has my trust.
I shall be bold with men
If Christ be pleased to assist.
I have a little faith.
I have a little lived by faith
And so I may be bold.
Therefore, in the fear and name of God,
Accomplish what you know
And have been told.

God told me a psalm last night:
'Lord, Thou hast been favourable to Thy Land
Thou hast brought back the captivity of Jacob
Thou hast forgiven the iniquity of Thy People
Thou hast covered all their sins
Thou hast taken away the fierceness of Thy Wrath
Tell us, o God, of our salvation

And cause Thine anger towards us to cease.
Wilt Thou be angry with us forever?
Wilt Thou draw out Thine anger to all generations?
Wilt Thou not revive us again
That Thy people may rejoice in Thee?
Let Mercy and Truth meet together,
Let Righteousness and Peace kiss each other.'

Earth is Heaven's dream.
This poor English earth
Is an emblem of Heaven
Where God's blessing is supreme
Where Falsity and Greed,
Cruelty, Sin, Fear
And all the Hell-dogs of Gehenna
Lie chained under our feet
In proper postures of defeat.
This is England, gentlemen, England
August and brave and sweet.
Other people see a little of the sun
But we have great lights.

May God invest you with His presence.
He made your hearts and mine.
Let Him live in His own creation.

God bless you all, my countrymen.

An Expert Teacher

'God's ways need not be justified' Oliver said.
'Protestants were massacred in 1641.
Those who might have made an Assembly of Saints died
By drowning, fire, strangling, sword and gun.
God ordained they be avenged.
At Drogheda, I saw His judgment executed
Upon these barbarous wretches
Whose hands were thick with innocent blood.
As well as that, God's judgment meant
Less blood would be shed in the future.
The sword is an expert teacher
Like a drowning cry or the smell of burning.
Blood shed in proper quantities prevents
More shedding. Men are quick at learning.'

Oliver's Wexford

'The soldiers got a good booty in this place.
There are great quantities of iron,
Hides, tallow, salt, pipe- and barrel-staves.
In the Fort, we found a hundred cannon.
There is likewise some excellent shipping,
Especially three Frigates of twenty guns.

Of the inhabitants, those who did not die
Ran away. Your coward always runs.

I wish an honest people would come and plant here.
There are fine houses, opportunities for trade,
Marvellous advantage in herring and cod.
The Town is strong, pleasantly seated
With an earthen rampart fifteen feet thick.
I am pleased to possess this Wexford. Thank God.'

A Request

The Secretary of the Irish Blood Donors Society
Wrote to Oliver for a contribution.
She said his blood was of rare quality
And would improve the prospects of lesser men.
She'd settle for a few pints, she said,
And entreated Oliver to do his best.
Oliver studied the letter at length, then replied
'Dear Madam, I do not bleed by request
And yet I do not wish to appear unaware
Of the plight of men of inadequate blood.
May I suggest you send somebody
To accompany me on my Irish Campaign?
I can guarantee a supply to meet your needs,
Bottled and labelled, if you wish. Yours sincerely…'

A Distinctive Note

Oliver's personal blood-bottler was a memorable sort,
Of a scrupulous disposition.
He brought blood-bottling to an enviable art
Yet never bragged. Rather did he meditate upon
Those men, women and children
Whose blood he had been chosen to bottle,
Musing on how the red stuff sustained each human
From birth-spasm to death-rattle.
In the matter of labelling, he had few equals.
As well as noting the type, he liked to add
A personal touch, a distinctive note
Such as 'This belonged to a stammering lad'
Or 'This priest had an aversion to bibles'
Or 'This good sister was bearded like a goat'.

Talk

'Talk! Don't talk to me of talk.
In this poor swooning slumberous mumbling canting age
His dialogue is rude and obsolete,
A thing of inexorable sweeping rage.

'As articulate orderly men,
Not as a blustering murderous kennel of dogs
Run rabid, shall you continue on
This earth. Are you men or earwigs?

'Talk! What is this wind called talk?
Here is a man whose represents a thing,
Who does what he says he will do.
Is there anything in this world but bluster?
Welcome, then, one who knows his own thinking,
A man for whom a word is a deed come true.'

Oliver to His Daughter

Dear Daughter, I write not to your husband,
One line of mine begets many of his.
This makes him, I fear, sit up too late and
Breaks his sleeping peace.
Seek to see your vanity, your carnal mind.
To be a seeker is next to being a finder.
To taste the Lord, first taste your sour self.
Who can taste Him, and go less in desire?

Dear Heart, press on. Let not your husband
Cool your love of Christ, but let the marriage-bed
Inflame your love of God's own Son.
Love most in your husband what bears the image of Christ.
Look on that, love it best, and all the rest for that.
There is no sweeter reason to love a man.

Shelter

The trek from Wexford was hell
For horse and Foot.
The roads sneered at the soldiers
Exhausted, cold and wet.
Imagine their relief, then, when they saw
The Black Abbey in the jaded light.
Oliver made no secret of his thanks to God.
A bed for the night.

But first, the horses must be catered for,
Gallant creatures patiently bearing men.
Off with their gear; bit, bridle, saddle, halter.
Into the church with them, shelter there
In sacristy and nave. Who'll complain
If they offer their dung at the High Altar?

Investing the Seed

The bulldog prowls around the house
The linnet fails in its cage
The three children sit still in a bedroom
'Be sure not to open the door'
Two gates leading to the house are locked
Scowling clouds subdue the sun
No one has laughed for a long time

There is work to be done

The man takes a bag of seed
Goes out into the fields
Invests the seed in the willing land
The woman shadows him, a mask on her face
She keeps looking around
A rifle in her hand.

A Memory

'At a signal from the sheriff the work began

The inmates of the cabins were dragged out on the road
The thatched roofs were torn down
The earthen walls battered in by crowbars
The women and children hauled out
And dumped on the stones
No struggle
It was soon over

It's a long time now but I still see that scene –
The sheriff on his horse
The crowbar brigade debauched but efficient
The memory of the evicted faces is pain
But these matters will take their course
If people won't pay the rent.'

The Cause

'All that we do is for religion.
Let apparitions be seen on the waters of Belturbet
And the drowned English rise crying at the moon
We do what we do for the love of God.
When we kill them, waking and sleeping,
Or strip them naked on freezing roads
Or let their guts festoon their feet
We do that work for the love of God
Who would not have us act another way
But orders us to burn all their houses
And whip the wretches to church for a good sermon
That they hear clearly what God has to say
On the matter of exposing their bodies to the shock
Of lying all night naked in the snow upon a rock.'

Connoisseur

The hand said, 'I'm a connoisseur of moments
And have been gifted with different skills.
I planted trees, got rid of weeds and stones.
When the time was ripe I picked apples.

Hedges, according to law, had to be kept
To a certain height. I was dutiful here.
I spancelled the barbarous summer, swept
Away the autumn. Land improved all over.

At home, I made electric cups of tea
Pushed a brush along the dependable floor
Watered chrysanthemums on the window-sill.

I coaxed milk from tired teats, I bundled hay,
I did accounts for a crippled auctioneer,
I changed nappies, I was in at the kill.'

Good Times

The hand said, 'I had some good times here
And there. I sliced bread and meat,
Lifted both to the appropriate mouth.
I belonged to a boy, I was all sweat
When he groped in the dark for Josephine.
I was cut, I caught a ball, I caressed
With increasing skill, sundry bums and breasts,
I sighed between thighs like the poor man
I belonged to. I greeted my own kind
Manfully. I wiped blood from a face, another's,
My own. I fought, I was raised in blessing,
I dug opportunist worms out of the ground,
I felt eyes on me saying, it wrinkles, withers.
True enough. What now? Hard to say.
Might write something.'

Snout

Far below me, I saw the planes like small
Plastic arrows petrifying the sky.
My eyes were radar. Right then, I knew all
About this base concealed from my allies
And me. My three African friends were astounded
And whispered to me that we might be seen.
We were. Suddenly, all four were grounded
Near the sea. Over our heads, this huge green plane

Appeared. The front of it was sneering,
A pig's glistening snout.
Out of its sides, three small planes hurled
Themselves above the clouds. The snout was trembling
When he towered, committed, and smiled out,
'I just want to give this little gift to the world.'

Tea

The photograph of the three pilots burned
From the bottom upwards, the Director
Explained why their three planes never returned
To base, the survivor grabbed the nurse's hair,
Hacked it off with a scissors and threw it
On the hospital floor. The day before
I'd seen the same thing happen to Brigid:
The moment I thought of her, I saw her.
I went up to her. I asked her if she'd
Take off her clothes. She smiled and said she would.
'Since my hair was chopped off I feel quite free.'
We lay together but somebody pushed me aside.
'Don't worry' he said, 'I'll soon have her covered
With what looks like my semen. It's only tea.'

Beyond the Warning Sign

The night I found true love is pollution
I went for a little jog on the beach.
I had a problem, there was no solution,
Or if there was, it prospered out of reach
Like a fly on a high marble counter
Mangling a speck of sugar with his front
Legs assiduous as a lover's fingers
Working the rich veins of bum and cunt.
I'd been told not to go too far without
A dog but, churned by my discovery,
I went God knows how far beyond the warning
Sign, lewd in Corporation red and white.
When the rats bunched, I had a god's body,
Escaped, slept well into the loveless morning.

Some Tiny Right

Night must have some tiny right to morning.
Brigid works in a suburban library,
Attends the occasional poetry reading
And, before bed, prepares her cup of tea
Or cocoa. I borrow books from her with
Religious devotion, can't read them. She
Flushes her distaste down my drooling throat.
I have plans for her. They'll fail badly.
Really, I have no right to my plans
Because her instinct for refusal is
Equalled only by my atrocious timing.
When she runs for a bus, it always rains.
As the bus sprays its elephantine piss
I stand there soaking it, stylishly waving.

Silver

All day long I stammered towards my room.
I kept it fixed and lucid in my mind.
All day long it rained and when the time came
For me to find the room, I could find
Nothing but rain. I must have circled The Square
A dozen times looking for the room
But all I could find was rain everywhere.
Yet the room was there because everyone came
For the silver moment in the life of Anne
And Edward welcoming all with a smile,
And Kitty showing a leg, flipping a song,
And John the butcher measuring beast and man
And myself, stupid with rain, astray while
Lilian spent all night wondering what was wrong.

Saskatoon

I've an address for Mum in Canada.
Somewhere in Saskatoon. I'm really bent
On seeing her again. Now that I'm a
Grown man, capable of a confident
Odyssey to even the remotest
Spot on this scarred earth, I have no hesit-
ation in going to knock at her breast,
To flay the dear exile with my whipwit.

I see a street, a house, a brass knocker.
I shall present myself as her baptised son,
Michael Patrick Gusty Mary Buffún.
I shall not descend to fool or trick her.
I'll use her in that style I've made my own
Although it's not my home ground, Saskatoon.

Wine

William of Orange barged into the room
In *Sunnyside* where Cromwell was resting
After chasing a fox from Mitchelstown
To Caherciveen, in vain. 'What's cooking?'
Barked Oliver, 'Why horse in here like that?
My bones are coming asunder after that chase
And the bloody fox escaped. Too much art
For these Irish hounds. But, William, what's this
Distress I see written across your face?'
'Oliver' sweated William 'I'm back from the Boyne
Where I drank deep draughts from victory's cup.
And yet, doubt chews my heart, I must confess.'

'Why should it?' queried Oliver.
                                    'Where's the wine?'
Croaked William, 'I think I've fucked things up!'

A Bit of a Swap

When the Pope came to Ireland, William of Orange
Was chosen by the two Houses of Government
To talk to the Pontiff on a wide range
Of subjects. William was subtle and blunt,
The right mix for a man who'd cope with the Pope.

'Holy Father' smiled William, mustering his intellectual forces,
'My chief concern is Irish industry. I hope
You'll like my suggestion about thoroughbred horses.
I understand you have a deep interest in bulls
And own, in fact, some choice Italian herds.
Swap bulls for horses, that's what I propose.'

The Pontiff ruminated: 'My child, your sales
In horses are about to soar. My word
On that. As for my bulls to you, who knows?'

78

Such a State

I have seen my friends in some very
Embarrassing positions, and my heart
Which is not sacred has bled for them
Albeit not at a rapid rate, and privately.
But I will never forget the sight
Of Oliver Cromwell in William Street,
Listowel. He was covered in shite.
I was struck dumber than usual. How greet
An old acquaintance in this public place
And he in such a state? No words that I
Could summon would have, at that moment, sufficed.
But then, from somewhere in Oliver's face,
Explanation dropped as from an addled sky:
'Buff, I have been floundering in the bowels of Christ.'

Uses

'I joined the St Vincent de Paul Society'
Oliver said, 'Because I was amazed
At the paralytic extent of poverty
In Ireland. It was worse in the old days
Of course, but let's not go into that now.
Man's basic problem is the same everywhere.
Not enough cash. I racked my brains to find how
I might get my hands on money to wage war
On the deprivations of the Irish poor.
Got it! Shift every cripple in the land
Into the streets. Stir the charitable juices
Of the bourgeoisie who need to exercise their
Pity. See them throw money on the ground
To join the cripples. Cripples have their uses.'

The Most Tattered Carpet

In through the wall breaks a child with Mum's face.
There should be dust in my hair, my nostrils.
None. Small laughing flowers adorn her blue dress.
Is this one of the forgotten people?
At my thought, she fingers the switch. Light is scorn
Powered to emphasise my ignorance.
Mum speaks, no, child speaks, 'Buffún, I'm unborn,
Don't look so stupid. Rise and let us dance.'

I have the most tattered carpet in this
Neighbourhood. Design is floral, faded beds.
I take her in my arms, dance on my knees,
Blue Danube first, *The Walls of Limerick* then.
She becomes all partners, women and men.
Laughs. Vanishes. My carpet is in shreds.

She Smiles Her Choice

I am constantly set upon by the dead
And unborn. The living I can cope with,
Dear friends, dear foes, material for canned myth
To be opened by someone with half a head.
I run my fingers on their jagged edges
And cherish their capacity to wound
Me. The dead have more power, more privilege.
Far out beyond noise, they make their own sound.
And the unborn press into time like a knock-
out blow into the heart of a canny fighter.
Tonight, this child insists she's my daughter,
Smiles into me so deeply I start to shake.
I beg her avoid the cars bearing down on her.
She smiles her choice as the cars roar nearer.

Master

'I am master of the chivalric idiom' Spenser said
As he sipped a jug of buttermilk
And ate a quaite of griddle-bread.
'I'm worried, though, about the actual bulk
Of *The Faerie Queene.* She's growing out
Of all proportions, in different directions.
Am I losing control? Am I buggering it
All up? Ruining my best intentions?
As relief from my Queene, I write sonnets
But even these little things get out of hand
Now and then, giving me a nightmare head.
Trouble is, sonnets are genetic epics.
Something in them wants to grow out of bounds.
I'm up to my bollox in sonnets' Spenser said.

The Position of Praise

'Praise God' said Spenser, 'You live where you choose,
Buffún. I'm not in love with Cork even
Though I enjoy all these pleasant Sundays
When I stand apart and watch the Corkmen
Lofting the viaduct. No, friends shoved me
Over here because I loved green tables
And round tables and gentle chivalry.
I would halt these coarse tides drowning
England but all a poet can be today
Is witness to ambitious ugliness
Disfiguring the old and graceful ways.
Since they have made an outcast of me
I know that I, in Cork, must always bless
Whoever mauls England. They maim. I praise.'

Stump

The page I was writing on became flame.
It set my hand on fire.
It said 'Buffún, I'll give you a choice –
Victim or martyr?'

'Thanks' I replied 'But could you lend
Me a bucket of water to quench my hand
And I promise I'll be your friend
Forever.' Page grinned, 'Burn on, Buffún, you'll find
It'll help you in the end.'

'The end' I yelled 'Is what I don't wish to know,
I love only what is beginning,
This trite belief keeps me alive.'

                           My hand
Burned as the page smiled, 'Buffún, you'll grow
Accustomed to your stump. Such sights are winning.'

Naked

I've had a few inspiring conversations
With the yellow wallpaper in my room.
Normally, speaking to folk, I'm lousy-cagey,
Even more idiotic than the next man.

This morning, the wallpaper surpassed itself
And all day long it has forced me to think.
'Buffún' it said 'you've put yourself on the shelf,
Your little soul is stained with Woolworth's ink.

Your trouble is you haven't learned to be
Naked. Old man, you're still swaddled in lies.
Strip them off, one by one, till you see all

Or nothing. Difficult? Just look at me,
Come here, strip and tear me as you please,
Then feast your eyes upon a naked wall!'

Plans

William of Orange was always worried
About the state of the Gross National Product.
'Unless the G.N.P. improves' he said
To a seminar in Listowel, 'We're fucked!

I've been looking around at this island
And it's clear to me the major industry
Is holiness. The people's souls are sound.
I note a link between holiness and money.

I'm drawing up plans for a factory
Where I shall manufacture rosary-beads.
About a million tourists blow this way

Each year to view our native sanctity.
God is telling us to use our heads.
Holiness is thriving, lads. Let's make it pay.'

Praise the Lord

'Let's get one thing clear' said Oliver, 'One thing alone:
My life's purpose is to praise the Lord
Whatever I have suffered, wherever I have gone,
No matter when or where I have warred
Against The Enemy, the hand
Of The Lord has always worked for me.
I saw Heaven's lightning descend on England
And burn up idle bluster in a night.

If I conducted a terrible Surgery
On some, I pity them. They are pitiable enough.
Yet The Lord's hand guided me right.
Whenever I killed, I killed from His love,
His hand in mine, His ways my ways.
For all I've done, I tender Him all praise.'

After Church

William of Orange is not a man
To let his mind blaze with excitement
Except under unusual conditions.
He understands the beauty of restraint.

But yesterday, after Church, he said to me
'Buffún, I'm going to strike an important blow
For Irish industry.
I know horses. I have a mare now

Second to none, trained at the Curragh,
Coming along so beautifully
I know that there has never been

A winner like her. Come to Cheltenham, my boy,
You'll hear the Irish roar of victory
When Blister Friggett rides the Faerie Queene.'

Souvenir

Enter Balder, light of our lives. He died.
His brother went to look for him
Through gloomy valleys, subterranean torrents,
Pushing downwards to the death-realm.

At Lonesome Bridge, on the River of Moaning,
An old vixen-eyed harridan kept watch.
The brother asked her if she'd seen Balder.
'Yes, Balder was here' wheezed the old witch,

'But he's gone North and down, forever down.'
The brother went after him, found him
In hell with the wife. They were a sad pair.

'Please understand' said Balder 'that I can
Never go back. Brother, hell is my home.
Good-bye. Take this used bulb as a souvenir.'

Looking for the Name

I saw myself crossing the bridge looking
For the name Balder said was my birthright.
I looked into the water, saw an eel twisting
Like a wish chasing itself through shade and light.

I came to the cross, an old man slept in
The sun Balder had promised he'd leave with
Us always (but he lied) and the cheap wine
The old man drank stank like a dead myth.

I explored a mountain of shredded tyres,
I poked about in a black ass's dung
Marvelling at the patience of the beast,

I tried the tongues of all my favourite liars,
I read books, heard yarns, listened to songs
But I found no name north south west or east.

Choice Specimen

'I am occasionally bothered by cries'
Oliver said 'And at the oddest times, too.
When, for example, I'm chasing butterflies
Through abandoned sandpits in Knockanore
Practically tripping myself up
In pursuit of this choice specimen
Fluttering six inches above my cap
Or sunbathing on an inaccessible stone
I hear, for no reason that I can say,
Cries as from some poor devil burning alive
In a town square, citizens looking on,
Profoundly interested, stirred to pity.
Then I hear nothing. There are no more cries
When my trusty net nabs that choice specimen!'

An English Jade

'There's an iron gate, a tree-lined avenue
And at the end of that a Big House
With a rent-fat master and mistress.
Here's what you must do.
Cut off his head, kick it on the front lawn
Like a football. Score clever goals.
Let the wife witness the head of her man
Making brave sport for trained rebels.
When you tire of that game, strip her.
Ring her body with ropes of straw.
Place his kicked head in her hands.
Set fire to her then. Let the fire
Inspire her. Unleash your applause
When the English Jade flames into dance.'

Actors

We are all actors here, who love our acting.
Captain Edward Adair
Honoured among us for his pronged bragging
Acted lavish parts among the rebels of Clare
Bringing the curtain down on the unrehearsed Irish.
Captain Adair found Ever Magee, an aged man,
In bed, killed him, fired his house
And swore 'By Christ, this old man can
Act no longer, a critical fire
Has brought a dire end
To his career.'
I forget how Captain Adair
Bowed out. Does it matter?
We are all actors here.

A Part to Play

'When will you know' asked Oliver, smiling,
'Even as you listen to tales of what I've done
To people when I revelled in wrecking
And killing, hacked flesh from bone
In lazy provincial towns, burned down
Whoever and whatever would not yield to me,
Pitched in the gutter some remarkable men,
Ignored what the innocent had to say,
Drove my own soldiers like beasts of burden
Through weather that would shrivel God's heart
Touched at the spilling of so much blood,

When will you know, poor sad-eyed man,
I had a part to play and played that part?

Given time, it will be all to your good.'

Cream

'That night, I pitched camp outside the town'
Storied Oliver, 'And hearing a great shout
Among the soldiers, I rushed and looked out
Of window. I spied a soldier with a churn
On his head. He had been purveying abroad
And found a vessel filled with cream.
At the tents, some got dishfuls, some hatfuls.
One fellow, wanting a modest drink, came
And lifted the churn to his mouth
But another, canting it up, it falls over his head,
The poor man is lost in it, finds no words,
The cream apparels him from crown to foot,
His honest head sticks fast in the tub.
I love an innocent jest' Oliver purred.

An Example

'In Limerick, the besieged Irish were all plague and famine.
Great numbers of people tried to abandon the town,
Sent out by the garrison as useless persons
Or to spread their contagion among us. Ireton
Commanded them to go back, threatened to shoot
Any that should come out in future. This
Failed. Ireton decided we should execute
Some, an example. I chose the only full-breasted
Wench in the bunch. Her father was with her,
Begged he be hanged instead of his daughter.
I said no. 'Up on the gibbet, lass. Mount! Mount!'
I hanged her in full sight of the town walls.
The gaping townsfolk were so filled with terror
We were no longer disturbed on that account.'

Not Born Yet

Holmes was there and Fairley
And Lieutenant Girders
With the polished stick.
He gave the orders.

It was he chose the houses
To be burned:
Bamburys', Collins',
Walshs', Finnucanes'.

The houses flamed all night,
Ashes by morning.
The polished stick flashed in the light.
'Let this be a warning.'

I was not born yet.
But I suffer it.

They Said Yes, It's There

He was there but would not come forward.
So were Mum and, after a while, Oliver
Advising a child not to be impertinent.
It was quiet at first but a certain stir

Buzzed when a local historian said
He ⌣ like to photograph the gathering.
His ultra-modern camera exploded
In his face as he stood in the room doing

His job. Bits of face slow-motioned down the air,
The child rushed to fit the pieces together,
This was a puzzle but he jigsawed well

Having more practice at that than at other
Games. The historian showed his face to Oliver
And Mum. They said yes, it's there. Like hell.

A Low, Whitewashed Wall

One by one, she leads us to the garden,
Xavier, Jeremiah, Mick, the others.
This fresh air should lighten my burden.
Have I ever counted all my brothers?

Never. No time to start now. Let them come
Into the garden where I often sweated
Taking time off, I must concede, to name
The different flowers in their cherished beds.

Whenever she wishes to pronounce, she
Stands on a low, whitewashed wall above
The lettuce. Fresh leaves, crisp hearts, slugs, earth-stains.

Death is an appetite, she says. All you
Darlings drink me and what you drink is love.
She looks down. Brothers. Nameless. Countless. Stones.

A Green Blanket, Folded

I was in the road outside, near Keane's door.
When I looked up I could see her in the bed
Beyond, now, the last reaches of the fever
That had preyed so hard she was a scavenged
Parody of herself. Bones, yes, there were bones
Sticking out, deliberate as paling-posts.
I saw her confabbing with other skeletons
And marvelled at the gaps where her breasts
Had been. The window began to darken.
A son slowed his body into the room
A green blanket, folded, in his left hand.
Inside me, the darkness started to harden
And I heard myself shouting up to him
'Let the blanket swaddle her body and mind.'

Whoever Is Laughing

There's a laugh, somewhere.
Rosaleen thumbs out her eyes.
'Here are specimens of the best native diamonds.
Wear them, please.

Need a break? Care to visit the land of the young?
Climb in through these two holes
And wander pleasurably among
Forgotten people.'

Her eyes are back there, now.
The laughter is a masterful sound.
I want to move. I cannot.
Whoever is laughing is crippling my hands,

Whoever is laughing is needling my brain
And shaping to dance with Rosaleen.

A New Animal

Rising finally into a beginning,
I walk.
The city is a new animal at night, resting
Through itself, aftermath of shock

While the laughing continues
In the river's eyes.
I might excavate the water,
Discover my peace

Written there in illuminated script,
Study the pages while the laughing
Scuds from quay-wall to quay-wall,

Torpedoes the innocent foreign ships,
Deepens at wrecked cargoes stuttering
Towards the sea, old man-swallowing ghoul.

A New Menu

I saw the giant, unfixed, tonight. I had
The gumption to ask him what he was doing.
'I've been fasting for a while now' he said,
'But soon I shall resume my diligent chewing.
The roof of your Parish Hall was succulent
But now I'm into Public Libraries,
Cathedrals, Jewellers, Antique Dealers,
Music Lounges, Electrical Supplies,
Tools, Plastic, Fittings, Quality Furniture,
Pet Stores, Fireplace Centres, Greeting Card Boutiques,
Economy Wallpapers, the Stock Exchange.

Assorted Warehouses, Banks and Funfairs
Guarantee I'll never get too weak.

Cities offer little beyond my range.'

Iron

If my sleep is a pool where my friends drop
Inquisitive stones, observing my dreams
Ripple out to extinction, I'll put up
With that. Friends have claims, though some be bums.
But it's quite another thing to bar my
Single window with long sticks of rusty
Iron and then with another bar to
Clang me where I lie, amateur and lusty.
Jack-rabbiting into the wall, I see
A Nissen hut in a spruce corner of Kent
Where a free poet pisses on glow-worms.
Midnight. The hut snores. An outraged black boy
Bangs the corrugated iron in complaint.
This clamour spreads to outlying farms.

One Who Loved Lightning

'You see, Buff' furied Oliver 'the Elysium
England has prepared for her heroes;
Dreariest continent of shot-rubbish the eye
Ever saw, lurid twilight as of the shadow
Of death, without index, without finger-post,
Gaunt solitude peopled only by pedants,
Dilettantes, phantasms, errors, nightmares,
Griffins, wiverns, suitable chimeras:

Under such monstrous lumber-mountains
Under the muck and ashes of generations
Under the stupidity and shame
At which the heavens themselves rail unvictorious
Under the dark belly bloated with contagion

There, waiting, one who loved lightning, I am.'

A Condition

Oliver is a blunt man,
Blunter than any fiddling poet can be.
He squatted outside the town,
Wrote a letter to the Enemy.

'Surrender, you may leave this place.
Resist, you're dead. Decision by return.
If you wish to see me face to face
Come to the Mass-rock outside the town.'

The two men met there. The defender
Would capitulate on one condition.
'A condition' he said 'that nothing can shake.'

'What? A condition?' roared Oliver.
In the burning of an eye he grabbed the man,
Smashed his head against the Mass-rock.

'Charge!'

William of Orange visited the Curragh
With a view to opening a stud-farm
And giving a fillip to Irish industry.
Looking across the plains, a warm
Look sunned his face like a summer afternoon,
Benedictus on the land from shore to shore.
'All beasts bred here would be prime flesh and bone'
Sparkled William, 'God! I can see their spoor
Like prints of power from here to the horizon.
With a team of jockeys led by Blister Friggett
All the races will be mine. Mine! By George!
I'll be a symbol, history's elected sign,
Me on a royal white stallion, looking out
Of a handsome kitchen-towel, shouting 'Charge!'

A Bad Winter

It was a bad winter and The Belly
Was worried about his pigs
Scraggy with hunger. He stood
And looked at them, he really took them in.
The Belly saw into the future like some god
Or prophet and did not like what he saw.
He bulged in home and counted his children.
He selected one son, a fatty boy,
Led him forth like an important father
Bossing some strange tale in the Bible
And threw him to the pigs. They ate him.
Thus did The Belly cope with the bad winter.
Killing-time came and saw him smile.
The pigs fattened in fair weather. He ate them.

Pits

'I came out of a pit, I went down into a pit,
I am a pit' the giant said, rubbing his eyes.
'It's all blood in the pit, blood groans and sighs
And throws up out of itself a spate
To cover the world and create me.
I listen to the battles going on inside
Me. There are no words yet for conquest or pride,
I'm a rough draft for what screams in eternity.
And the most ferocious thing in me is
This longing for a sleep I can't imagine,
A sleep so deep it could swallow the pit,
A sleep so long I could go countless ways
Through it, never ending, always just begun.
Here, in my blood-pit, I'm preparing for that.'

Stall

How did I blunder into that stall
Of cattle steaming in the autumn night?
I found myself there when the moon was full
And the smell of dung thronged me, bit by bit.
Light fell on the backs and bellies of cows
Lying close to each other in their own dung.
I was an outcast then, I had no house,
No parents, brothers, I was very young
And I had no one but the beasts to be with,
Feeling their breath about me in the dark,
Knowing each rump and hoof, sensing each head
Grow to stare at me through nightbreath,
Great eyes soft and stupid, horns stark
And curving long shocks through my blood.

Reading Aloud

Oliver Cromwell is a cultured man
Though he's not fond of the drama.
'Buffún' he said 'I once read all *The Faerie Queene*
Or, to be more precise, I tried to.
Spenser had a little estate down in Cork
And he found peace there, deep, unending,
Like his poem. But think of all the work
He put for years into these singing
Stanzas. That poem is one of England's glories.
Few Englishmen bother to read it now
Though much of it is still fresh as a berry
On a hedge in the middle of the Maharees.
I plan to spend next winter reading it aloud
To myself in my little estate down in Kerry.'

Spits

'Jesus Christ!' burst Cromwell, 'I saw this spit
Right in the main street of Caherciveen.
I nearly threw up at the sight of it.
As you may realise, I have seen
A few things to make any man throw up
But this black yellow slimy spreading heap
Of muck was, in any tongue, the last straw.
Even to mention it now makes my throat creep.
Yet, in spite of my disgust, which was deep,
I walked over to it and with my heel
Pressed and ground it into the blessed earth.
The earth swallowed it. What will earth not take?
I've ground men under my heel as well.
Men who are spits get from me what they're worth.'

Battlefield

I opened the boot of the old Baby Austin.
Evil gushed up at me
From a windowed envelope.
It thrashed down my mouth

Squatted in my heart.
I was a loud man, I roared,
My lips became an ape's,
I had no respect for any word

But howled at the crowd staring at me
In small groups on the road, a gaping
Amazement in their caged faces.

I became a battlefield when I
Found my ape's lips trying
To say, then saying, Jesus, Jesus.

96

Friends

Jesus is Oliver's friend, they get on well
Together despite the occasional
Tiff concerning the nature of pain
Inflicted on folk who lack the cop-on
To comply with Oliver's ironside commands.

Jesus spits out of the mouth of a cannon
Jesus squats on the hilt of a sword
Jesus trudges with the Foot through rain
Jesus makes a breach in the walls
Jesus turns a deaf ear to the women
Jesus stands in the streets of blood
Scratching his head, looking somewhat puzzled,
Jesus agrees this island needs purposeful men
And will memo that conviction to God.

Ash

Bat was gutting a rabbit in the back-kitchen
A Woodbine shrinking towards his lips.
His wife for the thousandth time
Was concentrating on potato-cakes.

When the fire started, I was sitting
At a mahogany desk, second-hand,
And should have run, but even allowing
For the fact that I'm a mind-

Less coward, I stayed sitting there, believing,
I think, that I had something to complete.
Looking back on it now, I still feel the lash

Of the fire's tongue as it began abusing
Bat, the rabbit, the wife and, lastly, me
Taking it all in, crouched lump of ash.

I'm a Man

I'm a man who scraped out of Liverpool
With four hundred and thirty-two others.
How long ago? How far? I only know
The retching smell of the dead before they're
Dumped at sea. I feel lighter all the time.
The waves repeat themselves like pains like
Dreams of bread and Indian meal and talk
Of relief from a man who reads the Bible
And is concerned. The voyage is almost over.
This land will supply new ways of looking back
At the cheated living and the relieved dead
Drifting in the sea's freezing fever.
I will scrape what can be scraped off any rock
Like a child nailing lice out of its head.

The Blood

The blood flowing from Homer's ears
Colours the sawdust in the timber-yard
Where trees roll in from Government forests.
The blood floods a blackbird's beak,
Enthuses through a drinker's tale
Of Aero Lyons in the caves of Clashmealcon,
Love for a sister, starve him out, the sea's howl
At the rope frayed or cut from a climbing man
Flung back like a doll to the rocks below.
The blood is flowing through the song a boy
Is trying to lock into his head
Never wanting for words to sing or say
To the living, 'If there's any life in the dead.'

Oliver's Purchases

'I went to a wake.
A woman was lamenting her man.
The bitch was crying too much,
Her tears easy as flattery.

"Will you sell the corpse?" I asked
"I'll give you thirty pounds."
"Dear God" she cried, "Would you bargain like that?"
"I'll give you forty pounds" I continued.

"No" she replied.
"I'll give you fifty" I said,
"Here's the money for the taking."
"I'll take fifty" she surrendered.

If the Irish sell their dead
Surely I can buy the living.'

The Gate

'Open that gate for me' Oliver said
To the monk. The monk opened the gate.
Oliver, horsed, rode through in style
Confident now he'd not be late
For that dinner appointment with
William of Orange.
'Thank you' he smiled at the monk.

'Thank you, gentlemen' the monk replied.

'Gentlemen?' puzzled Oliver, 'I'm alone
On this horse. Why "gentlemen" then?
I'm alone. That's as sure as Kingdom Come.'

'Look behind you' the monk said, 'At that man
With the signed parchment in his hand.'
Oliver looked. The Devil, coy at his bum.

Gas

The Devil fucked Oliver Cromwell
In a cottage at the edge of Birnam Wood.
He fucked his body first, then he fucked his soul
And after that they sampled each other's blood.
Nine months later, gas poured from Oliver's hole.
An ambitious Austrian corporal came and harnessed it
For the good of the European, white soul.
Certain desolate thoughts result from that.

A quick fuck in a cottage can change the world,
An infernal frolic can scuttle a king
And no cosy poet need ever write it down.

Was the Devil disappointed? Did he hoof
Home to hell and wank off, cursing
Oliver for his superior cunning?

Out of Bounds

'Devil-fucked Lord Protectors are out of bounds,
Oliver' smiled the Sacred Heart. 'It means I
Can't include you in my personal anthology
Of saints which includes the élite souls of many lands.
Instead, you're elected to a distressed eternity,
Subjected to atrocious smells and sounds
And touchings. Touchings, Oliver, of the best minds
Analysing your wee frolic in the
Birnam Wood episode. It's the devilgas
That worries them. Why did you fart like that
And boom forth such camp philosophy?
Lovers of hell give people the wrong ideas
Propagate heady rhetoric and wit
And, most sadly, sever themselves from me.'

Born Kings

'I have known born Kings' Oliver said
'Of stout natural limbs, who crowned themselves
By putting on their private hat and thinking
"God help me to be King of what lies under this.
Eternities are there, Infinitudes, Heaven and Hell.
All these I must conquer in what is called today."

The love of power is noble. Mark this well.
Accept the Godmessage when it lights your way.

Ignore, Buffún, all cackling geese and ganders
The clack of articles and human tongues
Timorous babblers prattling round the bend.

God's is the voice, yours are the answers,
Thou Shalt Not and *Thou Shalt* write clear and strong
That all may read. Or be my dumb, quack-ridden friend.'

Oliver to His Son

'I love you, you are dear to me, so is
Your wife but, my son, you have waxed fat,
You are grown thick, you are buried in fatness,
You have exceeded your allowance and that
Is bad, you fall in debt. If pleasure
Be made the business of a man's life,
So much cost laid out upon it, so much
Time spent in it, as rather answers appetite
Than the will of God with which I am familiar,
I scruple to feed this humour.
Remember this: you are my son, therefore be lean,
I will not support your voluptuous blood,
I will help you to clean your conscience,
I love you, I write as honestly as I can.'

Oliver on Fear and Love

Beware of a bondage spirit.
Fear is the heart of it.
The antidote is love
Of which no heart has enough.
The voice of fear is
'If I had done this,
If I had avoided that,
The world might seem all right.'
Love says: 'What a Christ have I
What a Father in and through Him
His Name is my heart's deepest cry
Without Him I am dumb.
What a Nature
Is my Father:
He is Love, infinite, free,
Saying "You shall not depart from Me".'

This commends the Love of God:
It's Christ dying for weak men,
Those whom other men call bad,
Sinners, poor worms, wretches trampled on.
What God has done
What He is to us in Christ
Is the root of all comfort known to man.
Only He is our perfect rest,
In Him, we have done with falling,
No longer lost, severed, lonely.
This is our high calling.
Rest we here, and here only.

Grinning

The skeleton lay down beside me
And began to speak of family distress,
How brothers nurture brothers' jealousy
And sisters ram each other with malice.
Two dogs bounded into the room
And copulated at the foot of the bed;
The skeleton and I considered them
Not caring who was alive or dead.
The sated dogs barked their contentment
And the skeleton, turning randy, turned to me.
I was suddenly dumb.
Then, 'No!' I yelped. The skeleton knew what I meant
And faded into flesh, packed flesh, gradually
Becoming the body of my grinning Mum.

Workers

'Divers British employed by the Irish
(for at that time the Irish would none of them work)
Were, after they'd sown and cut and threshed,
Murdered. I was dead too, had not dark
November helped me escape to a friend.
The names of the dead drift like living
Figures, pleading, pleading, across my mind.
Night and day, the names keep moving:
James Hunter, John Key, Andrew Sloane,
Peter Black, Sanders Ross, Charles Beard,
William Harpur, Michael Gardiner, Nicholas Wall,
Arthur Hill, James Traill, Robert Braine,
George Rawden, Henry Garvin, Jeffrey Caird;
Forgemen, smiths, carpenters, workers all.'

Discipline

'You know your Irish tragedy, Buff?' queried
Oliver, 'It's this: you have no discipline.
Discipline cannot be rushed or hurried
But is a problem of moulding men to my vision
Of them. Can an Irishman be properly moulded?
Your common Englishman can, admirably so.
I moulded an army of disciplined soldiers.
They fought well. When the day came for them to go
Back to the world, they kept their discipline.
Of all that army, not a man begged in the streets.
This captain turned shoemaker, this lieutenant a baker,
This a brewer, that a haberdasher,
This common soldier, a porter; each man in his
Frock and apron, disciplined, an English worker.'

Oliver's Prophecies

'I will be remembered as a killer of language,
As Coppernose, Rubynose, Nose Almighty.
Before the battle of Worcester, in a fit of rage,
I will sign a pact with the Devil
Using the blood from the little finger
Of my right hand. He will give me seven years
To do my work. I'll do it. I'll be the centre
Of blame, the heartbeat of hate, the focus of fear.
I'll stable horses in St Canice's Cathedral,
I'll be a farmer, a brewer, a shoemaker,
I'll have a portrait of the Devil on the wall
Of my bedroom. Each night, exhausted, I
Will pass the portrait. It will smile and bow and say
"Dear Noll, we'll never part company".'

Entertainment

Oliver said, 'Come, Buffún, tell me a joke.
Badly do I need a laugh, being tired of triumph.
Conquest is grim, 'tis but a kind of rack
On which my mind is stretched from dawn till night.
So come on, perform for me. Here's a biscuit-tin,
Stand up on it, paint your face, hump your back,
Dear Fatuus Homunculus Hibernicus. A feast of wit
Is what I need. Let me laugh away this rack.'

I hopped on the biscuit-tin, Boland's Crackers, in fact.
'Oliver' I said 'I'm your doctor. You're sick.
You have five minutes to live.' 'My God' howled Oliver,
'Five minutes! Is there *anything* you can do for me?'
'Perhaps' I opined 'I could boil you an egg.'

'Thou cod' stormed Oliver, 'Hand me my whip. Bend over!'

The Learning of Pity

There is hate in the child's eyes
For his father's father
Who prowls the house half-naked late at night
Looking for whiskey and a little water.
The whole house is changing
And the child's eyes are progressive.
The old man knows what's in the air
And seems hardly disposed to forgive.

What did Oliver's son think of him?
What does any son think of any old man
Withering away, shanks thinning, eyes rheumy,
Hands trembling, speech foolish? Yet this is the custom
And strangely there are those, even the occasional son,
Hurt and renewed in the learning of pity.

Honest-to-God Oliver

I asked Oliver what he did for sex
During his Irish campaign.
'Sex' waxed Oliver 'Is blood
Spitting from the sky like rain
On the heads of stupid people.
Sex is my men storming the walls
Of a town before breaking and burning.
Screams of surrender tickle my balls.
Flames shooting up from a Catholic spire
Make a noble erection. Flesh warms to see
Superstition gutted and wrecked.
Anarchy hanging for crows heats my desire.
Streets choked with rebel blood stimulate me
And women, run-through, are properly fucked.'

A Sick Business

If that Buffún asks me any more questions
Particularly those of a personal nature,
Mused Oliver, I'll cut his bloody throat.
He's such a squalid, inquisitive creature
He never knows when to draw the line
But goes on prying like a nagging woman
Scraping away at the inside of my mind
Lusting after any scrap of information.

I dislike having to answer questions
And when this mere prick of a Mick
Looms like an Inquisitor before my eyes
Expecting swift answers, instant revelations,
I know that communication is a sick
Business. Complete silence is completely wise.

Performance

'I was on dexedrine during my entire
Irish campaign, Buffún,' Oliver said,
'That, and this recurring sliver of a Bach cantata
Tripping through my head
Kept me from going Irishmad.
I could walk forty miles a day
So long as I popped some pills along the way.

Could I work miracles in Ireland? I did.

But Jesus, Buff, the effect on my hormones
Was something to behold. I was up to it,
I could perform, part the whisker, bury the bishop, do the trick,
Striding among those dying groans and moans
I composed limericks, epigrams of detonating wit
Concerning the performance of my not ignobly proportioned prick.'

Lettering

I belong to that silent majority
Who do not write letters to *The Irish Times*
But I swear to Christ I felt like writing
This morning when, on getting the 16A
And lurching through the city
Of Parnell, O'Connell, Emmet, Grattan,
I saw, scrawled on a wall in red lettering,

BOOM WENT MOUNTBATTEN!
            (Signed: Loving Care.)

I'm a quiet sort, not given to
Public explosions of private indignation,
I keep my cool, I do not give vent,
I brood on the good, the beautiful, the true,
I deplore murder, I quote Pearse and Tone,
I want to say what a patriot is, I can't
                        (or won't).

Ass

A proper donkey will do any kind of work.
So Neddy-Ned-Ned, a black ass, a thoroughbred
Of more than Christian fortitude,
Was led from his stable at midnight
In the midst of a well-earned snooze,
Tackled to his cart, driven seven miles
To where a young man lay dead
Shot through the head for his political views,
Loaded with the corpse, urged back through rain
And wind to...O let's say to the corpse's home
Where the willing beast was relieved of his burden
Only, next morning, to be tackled again
To that inevitable cart, this time
To drag dung to a promising garden,
So promising, indeed, it suggested Eden.
            To beat an ass to death is a man-mean feat
And that is what happened to our thoroughbred
Who'd played his part in the fight for freedom
And should have been ranked among the glorious dead,
Young flowers on his grave, hot prayers being said,
Our leaders, eyes heavenward, wishing him at one with God.
Instead, what, my brothers, do we find?
Just one more forgotten hard-working ass
Without epitaph, biography or ballad
Or portrait or parade or rosary or commemorative Mass.
Yet many beasts are remembered with love
Including dogs, cats and the odd prize-winning horse
But not yon black Trojan that gave
All. Halt a while, traveller, and spare a thought
For the true worker, true patriot, Neddy-Ned-Ned.

Radio

The otherness of God hits me like icy rain
Or like that babble of European
Accents dancing from wall to wall when
I'm gregarious enough to turn the radio on.

An old creamery-manager left it to me in his will.
It has a brown snout, wrinkles and black knobs
That plug you in to any studio hellhole
Of your choice. It harangues my skull, chest, ribs

Like the voice of God banging Moses what to do
When his randy band surrendered to havoc
In their sweaty groping through excessive sun.

My creamery-manager measured milk justly
Every morning. Moses, I hear, came unstuck.

The otherness of my radio bleeps me alone.

The Load

I want this load blasted off my shoulders.
What is it, anyway? The weight of a mistake?
A hard hand poised, deciding when to strike?
Or one of the old familiar boulders
Like a certain mouth pushing its noises
Through my head and heart until
My blood can do nothing but spill
Itself on the ground at my feet? It flows
Down Main Street into the river shuffling
To the sea like myself to school
And questions about natural resources, God,
History, X and Y, parsing. A man is teaching,
My back sweats, I listen, his voice is full
Of itself, the air bids me bear the load.

System

'It's not enough to demoralise; we must degrade.
Let's deprive them of elective suffrage, exclude
Them from corporations, magistry, the bar,
Bench, juries, vestries. They cannot be
Sheriffs, solicitors, gamekeepers, constables.
They cannot have arms. If they have a gun, whip them.
If they have a horse worth five pounds, take it from them.
The law cannot suppose that any such person
As an Irish Catholic can be said to exist.
Listen, the mere Irish do not exist,
The world will know they do not exist,
These Irish must never go to school,
Offer ten pounds for a Popish teacher's head,
If Paddy believes he exists, poor Paddy's a fool.'

Delight

'Ed Spenser is a great lad for beauty'
Nodded Oliver, 'He has devoted nights and days
To pleasuring his fellow-countrymen.
Therefore, say I, he deserves all praise.
I mean, Buffún, just glance at this nasty world,
Look at the ways these humans treat each other.
You'd swear to God that men were bloody apes
Or worse, the way brother murders brother,
Towns are flattened, women and children killed,
Great Houses gutted, the Word of God betrayed,
Satan enthroned, all virtue put to flight.
Aren't we lucky, then, to have such a skilled
Poet, one who has truly learned his trade
Of delight, delight, delight?'

In the Sea

Big Island whispered to little island
'I'm right here at your back.
Shall I bugger you?
Shall I breathe down your neck?
Most of the time I hardly see you at all
You're so small, you're so small
And when you insist that you really exist
I can scarcely follow your voice.
Well, do you exist, you sea-shrouded mite?
Or are you a floating illusion
Invisible to all except me?'

Little island replied 'There is sea-light
Between us, and storms and countless drowned men.
Yes, I'm near you. Near. Right here. In the sea.'

A Wound

Little island whispered over his shoulder
To Big Island who was reflecting on
The fact that there was no island more
Beautiful than himself, 'I'm here, and someone,

Probably one of my aboriginals,
Has set out in a low boat bearing proof
Of this. You may boot him in the genitals,
Work him over, lock him up, but his love

For me is such he believes I exist
And wishes to remind you of that truth.'
A bomb mashed Big Island in the side,

The aboriginal was duly booted and later lost.
'I'm here' said little island. 'I can see that'
Groaned Big, 'I must tend this wound before it goes bad.'

To Start With

'We are a poor country' the General said
Lifting a glass from the mahogany table
Sipping creatively in the hot atmosphere
'And we must improve it, as far as we're able.
Clearly, this is a matter of example.
Killings, for the most part, must be at night.
Choose, from the dissidents, one eminent sample.
Go to his flat. Say nothing. Take his life.
Take the corpse then, cut off the fingers
And the genitals, stuff the whole
Mess into the mouth.
Put the corpse in a sitting position somewhere
In the main street of the Capital.
Let's have fifty thousand such, to start with.'

Beans

The day after the world ended, I ven-
tured out to my local Supermarket
Where I'd bought many a can of Batchelor Beans.
For these beans I've long been a sucker but
It's their juice that really turns me on.
If I ever drink blood, I'd like it boiled
To this cool hue of your left-over man
Sniffing the riff of the post-world world.

There are bodies everywhere, the stink is
Worse than one finds in most conversation,
Fields are sores, every house a sad heap,
Each road a burst vein pouring blood and pus.
Still, to be fair, I consider the scene
Hardly equals what I have glimpsed in sleep.

Offenders

'Your aboriginals keep sticking thorns in my side'
Complained Big Island to little island.
'I'm sorry about that' said little island
'But what shall I do to stop them being bad?'
'My idea' said Big Island 'Is to build
A prison big enough to house all offenders.
When they do wrong and I establish their guilt
I'll send them there for a chastening number of years.'

'And where will this prison be?' queried little island.
Big Island smiled, 'Close to your heart, of course.
Even the worst offenders will feel happy there
Listening in respectful loving silence
To the heartbeat every aboriginal heart adores.'

Little island thought 'Why do I feel like an offender?'

It Is the Nearness That Kills

It is the nearness that kills, thought little island,
And Big Island is too near,
So near, it makes the sea a servant,
Calls rebellious waves to order
And eats me with its nearness.
And yet, it does not see me at all.
If I were farther away, if there were distance
Between us, Big Island might take a full
Look at me and see me for what I am.
But damn it, that's the prob, what am I?
Poisoned lake? Lost river? Buried forest? Bottomless bog?
People cry and die in me all the time,
Children change in me, birds eat me,
I am too far from myself, too near to Big.

A Solution

'My dear chap' said Big Island to little island
'You're a pest.
I can endure you when you're silent
But when you prattle and scrap you're the noisiest
Mite in the sea. You're a problem
And I've been giving sustained thought
To a solution. It may sound grim
To you but this vast expanse of water
Will be unlivable if I don't deal
With you. I'm going to cut off your head
And having chopped it I intend to keep
It. The rest of your body I shall
Donate to yourself. Treat it well. Don't be sad.
Be reasonable. You bore me when you weep.'

Good-Midnight, Ass-Face

I'm making the hell of an effort to think
Tonight, I think, but what's the use when one
Of my old friendenemies, Oliver, Mum,
He, Ed Spenser down in Cork or even
Balder and the wife in hell, a locked spot
From which, as you well know, there's no escape,
Just sit on your damned ass and take the rap
Of knowing if your hell is cold or hot
Or tepid,

           insists on crashing through my
Mind and throwing my little thoughts about
As wind kicks paper in a paper-chase
So that, all casual bedlam restored, I see
My mind is a mirror for a dimwit.
Bravely, I peer in. Good-midnight, Ass-Face.

Nothing Now

I do not want this dream but it dreams me.
No shoes, no shoes, she cries and dances
Among those who were once her sons
But now would nail her with crucifying glances
As her breasts dismiss each lover, wife and daughter.

I sold the land, one son insists, at the price
You suggested. She laughs her scorn and in her
Eyes I see a forest of raging ice
And I am walking there among the trees
And every human bond I ever made
Is melting in the branches jetting flame,

On, on to where she stumbles, falls, freezes
Into an appointed, perfect grave
And I am nothing now and never had a name.

Bits

I see the big Wexfordman tied
Like a knocked ox to the wooden frame.
His lips freeze but his eyes cry
As the Belly in uniform globes above him,
Smiling, the cat-o'-nine-tails in his hand.
'Your own name first, then all the others,
Else taste this government on your back.
Name after name now – the conspirators.'

I've often wondered how close flesh is to bone.
The Belly cracks the cat to show me how
Lashed flesh reveals deep bone, shreds red and warm
To earth. Bits of the big Wexfordman
Hear the lips left on his body say
'No more! No more! I'll inform! I'll inform!'

Such Stories

'I have such stories, such stories' cooed Oliver.
'George Preston, with two of his fellow soldiers,
Without leave from their Officer,
Went into the country to kill pigeons.
Finding none, they shot at a cock and killed it.
The woman who owned the cock came and claimed it.
'I want my cock, I want my cock' she cried
And followed the soldiers through the countryside

Choiring 'I want my cock, I want my cock'.
'Here's your cock' laughed Preston and cocked his gun.
'You tough old bird, pray take this cock from me.'
He shot the woman in the face and neck.
She died. George Preston was a cocky man.
I hanged George Preston from a tree.'

Revenge

Long have I studied the nature of revenge
And find it much to my taste. This morning
I picked up a seagull grounded by last night's storm
But the beaten thing had no wish to avenge itself
So I introduced its head to the rocks
Where I was foraging for dillisk and winkles
Propelled, as ever, by this electric sense of wrong
That I cannot define but cherish, nevertheless.

I have an enemy somewhere, that's for sure.
Does he sip whiskey on mindless evenings?
Insist on a fortnight's holiday each year?
Observe the sad gap between rich and poor?

Let him dither and dodge, he's in for a gouging
When I find him. But who is he? And where?

A Relationship

'Cromwell' I said, 'If our relationship
Is to develop, there's something I must tell
You, something from which I can't escape.
I hate and fear you like the thought of hell.
The murderous syllables of your name
Are the foundation of my nightmare.
I can never hate you enough. That is my shame.
Every day I pray that I may hate you more.
A fucked-up Paddy is what I am. Right?
Wrong. My loathing is such I know
I'll never rest.'

Oliver smiled. 'I sympathise with your plight,
Buffún. Understandable. You're fine, though, so
Long as you get it off your chest.'

'You really are an understanding
Son-of-a-bitch, Oliver' I replied
'And when this nightmare is over
And I understand why I have hated
You, your language, your army and your Christ
Who suffers your puritan crap
When he should bleed your guts into the sun
Or rip your heart out or break your neck
Or manacle you forever to a rock
Or stuff the barrel of a gun
Up your arse or assassinate your prick

Then we shall sit together
Outside a pub on a June afternoon
Sipping infinite pints of cool beer.
I have been brooding on this, mulling it over,
Our destinies are mingled, late and soon.
But the prospects are not good, I fear.'

Oliver to a Friend

All things work for the best.
You wish to hear of me. I am the man
You have always known, a body of death and sin.
I struggle to be honest
As I exalt the Lord and abase the flesh.
I have seen the Lord, I have prevailed,
I share the good-will of Him who dwelt in the Bush,
I am not deluded by this world.
You are troubled. Call not your burden heavy or sad.
If the Father laid it on you, He intended neither.
Go evenly through foul and fair weather
And know all fleshly reasoning is a trap
To make you say 'heavy', 'sad', 'pleasant', 'fine'.
Dare to be human; you'll be divine.
Dear friend, I dare to speak of spirit,
Such spirit as the world fears to know.
Quit your fleshly reason, seek to touch
The mind of God shown in the chain of Providence.
I say again, submit, let that spirit teach you,
The spirit of counsel and of might,
Of wisdom and the fear of the Lord.
He will lead you to what pleases His eyesight.
If you fail, good heart, to bear your burden well
You shall hardly bear the burdens of others.
I have done, I, a poor looker-on
At the workings of that spirit in this world.
Suffering? Men bring it on themselves.
Therefore, be fearless. My soul loves you, young man.

There Will Be Dreams

'Oh yes, there will be dreams' Oliver said
'Be assured, there will always be dreams.
And there will be men, willing makers
And willing destroyers of governments and homes.
I walked the bank of the Cashen this morning
And I stood watching at the edge of the tide.
I saw the Ballyduff men turn to their fishing
And every man of them was humble and proud
In his dreaming, touching what he knew to be
True in himself. I saw the boats heading out
And I knew why my life is a long war.
Any man will kill who has known the land's beauty
And though his heart suffer stabs of doubt
This land is a dream to be damned and saved for.'

Nothin'

A man in a ragged coat slouches into a shop,
Peers his beaten sadness around the place.
'Bread or blood! Bread or blood!' – five thousand
People cry at the gates of Listowel Workhouse.
The shopkeeper, Miss Mary Bridget Trant,
Apparitions from her kitchen on the right:
'Well, my good man, and what is it you want?'
'I want five shillins for to bury a child.'
'I'm sorry' she replies, 'There's nothin' to give,
Nothin' to beg, borrow, loan or squander.'
A final fire rebels in the man's bones.
Reaching inside his ragged coat, he lifts
Out a child's corpse, dumps it on the counter,
Makes for the shop-door, looks nowhere, runs, runs.

Famine Fever

It has, in fact, nothing to do with hunger.
It is a matter of lice.
The louse catches the disease itself
When it drinks the blood of a human who is
Infected. The bacteria multiply quickly
And deposit their excreta in the body.
Brush against a man bearing infected lice,
You pick up one yourself. You may, in a trice,
Inhale it, for it dries to an exquisite powder.
The bacteria enter the bloodstream through the lungs,
Eyes, or tiny cuts in the skin.
Quick as a tick, you're a victim.
Also, you too infect your own lice.
That is how the cycle begins again.

The Visit

To get the people's minds off disease and death
We organised a visit from the Queen.
She landed in Cork in the royal yacht
And continued by sea to Dublin.
There was a banquet at the Viceregal Lodge.
Her Majesty held a royal *levée* at which some
2000 people were presented, and a *Drawing Room*
At which 1700 ladies were accorded the same

Privilege. But the noblest scene of all was
The military spectacle in the Phoenix Park
In which 6000 troops took part.
'This is great' glowed Her Majesty, 'This is truly great.'
We considered the visit a resonant success
Though the poor went on dying at their usual rate.

My Indifference

'I never saw people so indifferent *to life; they continued
in the same berth with a dead person until the seamen or
captain dragged out the corpse with boat-hooks. Good God!
What evils will befall the cities wherever they alight?'*
    – The Chief Emigration Officer for Quebec

When that brave sailor sank his boat-hook
Into me, I was more dead than ever before.
Not even being hoisted aloft like
A bag of spuds and dumped in the water
Had the teeniest effect on my indifference.
I sank to the bottom with a sodden mind
And lumped there, stone-like, the Paddy dunce
I am. Slowly, as I defleshed, I found
My bones were of a sprightly nature
Apt to romp and frisk on the sea-floor
Frolicking as in a happy dream.
If I could only get myself together
Now, I'd rise to work and love once more.
O bless for me a candle and float it down the stream.

A Fiery Draught

In Ireland, few escape the country sickness.
To counter this disease
The natives use a remedy
Common and easy to be had,
A certain excellent liquor
Called uisquebagh,
A fiery draught
That wages war
On those sad ills that reign
Epidemically in this kingdom,
Not sparing natives more than strangers.
I see men, or those who look like men
Reeling from sickness-home to sickness-home
Mumbling, cursing, inflamed with helpless anger.

And the Curse Assumed Power

The spuds blackened
The wheat languished
The poems were buried in pits of silence
The music sagged and vanished
The women sneered at love
The children became hunger
The priests saw evil everywhere
Daylight was fear

And the curse assumed power over us all
Standing together there where seven roads meet
Able to define nothing but feeling the hurt
Of the words that clawed back off the sea
Because the sea couldn't suffer them to live in it:

'Scrios Cromwell ort.'*

*The Curse of Cromwell on you.

Who?

I see a man standing on a hill.
He sees a landlord on a horse. The landlord
Snaps at a young man on the roadside
'Tip your hat to me or you'll feel
This whip across your back. I'll see your blood
Corrupt the dust.'
                    The young man grabs the whip,
Beats the landlord to the ground.
                                        I see a ship,
A burning house and haystacks, an old man dreaming
In Chicago, out of touch, no records kept
Of names or deeds, his heart longing for a true
Picture of this man standing on a hill
Sayinng over and over 'Mike O'Brien, Mike O'Brien'.
A name on a hill somewhere. A man. Who?

Points

Where the tinker-girl with the scar on her forehead
And the tattered blanket wrapped around her left hand
Leaving the right free to work among wallets and pockets
Of tourists admiring the chief city of the island,

Pleads and preys, remembering her father's words,
'Come back empty-handed tonight and
You'll get my boot up your arse, love!'

You can still see, on the old buildings, marks
Where the bullets made their points to the walls
And the tall man's rhetoric linked
Pliant slaves like me to an angry God.

The fleeced tourist groans. The girl is gone.
Tonight, at least, she knows she won't be kicked
Though brothers wade knee-deep through brothers' blood.

More Caves

It was the scoriveen, treacherous weather of the cuckoo.
The lorries came rattling with oil
And petrol and what the people said was sulphur.
The soldiers poured oil, tar and petrol
Into hay and turf and flung it all, flaming,
Down to the cave.
                    A blaze roared, blackyellow
Smoke twisted and poured as the sea came bulling
The rocks. Looking down, I thought I saw
Rocks like bits of fat melting in a fire
But I didn't see men, like snakes,
Crawl out from the cave, over the boulders,
Between the pinnacle and the cliff, out of the creek
To the flat rock where hung, they knew, a ledge
They would climb to find more caves, more caves.

123

They Are One

The mountain people bring the mountain's sorrow
In their worked faces awkward in the town
As they shuffle after the coffin
Hearsed and rehearsed from corner to corner,
Over three bridges, into the open road
Leading to grass and nettles and a notion of repose.
The mill-women follow, fierce with grief,
Thin children straggle with dogs at the edges,
A crop of farmers at the centre, revenge in their blood,
The townspeople then, wave after wave,
A piled, anarchic tide
Conspiring in the back rooms of their passion.
There are priests, a few deserters, fishermen,
Old soldiers, labourers, men who own nothing.
They are one. There is nothing in the coffin.

Angers

The terrible incestuous angers of Ireland
Ganged up on me then
In the shadow of the Grattan monument
In the drab heart of Dublin.
Or did this happen somewhere in England?
A cement factory? A pub? Chiswick High Road?
Wherever it was, the angers ringed and harried me.
I thought I had died
And was looking down on these mad absences
And presences prowling cities, prowling minds
To lash and smash them to smithereens
Until all the living became shaken ghosts,
The future a prison crammed
With cowed nobodies and stammering haven't-beens.

Gravel

The soldiers had strong ropes and electric cord.
Each prisoner's hands were tied
Behind his back. His arms were tied above the elbows
To those of the man on either side.
Their feet were bound together above the ankles,
Their legs were bound together above the knees.
A rope was passed around the nine.

The soldiers moved away.

The prisoners' backs were to the mine.
When it exploded, the sudden hole in the road
Said nothing of our loss
And instead of singing in the dawn
Birds pecked the flesh off the trees
At Ballyseedy Cross.
Yet one prisoner escaped. He said 'Goodbye, lads' as the mine
Exploded, then he was on his hands and knees
In the road. Finding he was a whole man,
Free though burnt, he ran for the ditch, through trees,
Across the side of a hill, over a river, ran
Till he came to a sheltering house.
There was a girl. While he lay, she picked gravel
Out of his body.
           He has gravel in him to this day.

For months then he stole from house to house,
Sleeping in dugouts, hearing the midnight rain,
Waiting for bullets in the back and head.
They never came. He kept moving though,
Stayed clear of his own place for a long time.
He went home in the end. They took him in.

Three Tides

In our very own little civil war
The sea, as employed by some, is an exemplary weapon
Combining an ability to finish a job
With a reliable style of humiliation.
Proper use of such elemental efficiency, however,
Is available only to those who know
The sea's judicial character
In its constitutional ebb and flow.
As it approaches the shore
It nudges, first, a shy, frothful poison
Reminiscent of the slime on dying lips
Prior to that rattle that can still
Shred even the most knitted family
And cause fretful speculation about a will.
This is a slow poison, rhythmically, sensually slow.
Perhaps the stimulating moon
Quickens the pace because our law-abiding sea
Accelerates like a well-executed plan
Of dependable drowning waves, inexorable as generations
Of a fertile Catholic family true to God's
Randy laws, coming, going, coming, going, like sons
And daughters to work or hell or money or England or spawning beds.
Properly judged, a man buried up to his neck in the shore
Will take three tides to die. His brothers (mine too) say
This gives him time to meditate on his mistake
In taking the wrong side in that most uncivil war.
Unlike our manly land, our sea has never lied.
My father drowns to the moon's laws, head to one side.

Mud

Then I saw all the bodies becoming mud
Like philosophy or my best attempts to speak and sing
Of the generating works of God
Manifest in men, women and children becoming
Mud:
   and I see this toothless man
Taking a narrow path through a cornfield
Beating a goatskin drum in the morning sun.
Dozens of concerned faces come to see
And offer food to the man who tells them they are mud
Singing:
   'Let our prime boys and beautiful girls know
They are mud in the hands of the makers of pots and plates
And cups at their lips on wine-happy nights
And walls between neighbours to challenge the wind
And the makers themselves are mud when the same winds blow
Like thoughts like old coats wrapped round a freezing mind.'
   Do you blame me, then, if on certain days
I tend to see my friends as articulate lumps of mud?
At such moments, I grow intolerant of lipstick
While fashions in clothes and writing almost cause me
To scream in the streets. How pay proper homage
To the best-dressed Mud of the Year? Yet there have been
Distinguished lumps of mud such as Oliver and Ed
Spenser down in Cork stanzaing his Queene
Despite the afforested natives threatening to drive him mad.
The buried fertility of mud is thrilling:
Disciplined armies are stirring underground,
Sound chroniclers, critics, advocates of the life to come,
Scrupulous creators of new styles of killing
And a youngster, awakening to the people of his mind,
Flexing his fingers to play a goatskin drum.

Gusto

The Catholic bombed the Protestant's home
The Protestant bombed the Catholic's home
The Protestant castrated the Catholic
The Catholic castrated the Protestant
The Protestant set fire to the Catholic Recreation Centre
The Catholic set fire to the Protestant Recreation Centre
The Catholic cut the tail of the Protestant dog
The Protestant cut the tail of the Catholic dog

The Protestant hanged the Catholic
The Catholic hanged the Protestant
As they dangled like dolls from the freshly-painted
Protestant and Catholic gibbets
They held hands in mid-air and sang
With spiritual gusto, 'Onward, Christian Soldiers!'

Logic

Granted, I know nothing and when I hear
Of the death by a thousand cuts
Of a man hanging upside down
In a barn outside a small country town
And of the long pleasure my fellows find
Boring holes in another fellow's head,
Careful, mind you, not to touch the brain,
I hesitate to pray for the dead
But skulk instead in dark fields clear of the living.
Screams inhabit me by modest moonlight,
I am trying to walk, I can only fall,
I am become a specialist in falling
And as I hit the earth forever, I note
The black, tragic logic of it all.

The Right to Happen

Then the graves exploded
And the acquitted boys of ages
Elated from the judgment of clay.
Stylishly the grass parted
For the elected girls in their prime.
Nothinng can stop what has the right to happen.

So they danced, they danced.

The sky gives its verdict. The earth is not to blame.

There is nothing that is not in the present tense
And forever and not at all. This is a cage like a heart.
To walk from one cage to another is an endurable journey.
One is at least a spectator at the dance,
Couples will pair off, some will make another start,
I am the enduring witness of this hopeless-hopeful way.

A Threat

'The Irish are a threat to the health of the English.
There are thousands of these unfortunate louts
Stinking in our cities like rotten fish.
Their diet is poor, their dirty habits
Beyond words. They've brought their country ways to town,
They store up manure which they keep for sale
They have pigs and donkeys with them in their homes
But the most alarming practice of all
Is "waking the dead" when some Paddy has died.
A wake is little more than a drinking orgy
In the presence of the corpse. This might be harmless enough
But it takes them days to gather money for whiskey
And meantime the body is unburied.
Have these Irish no dignity? Where is their pride?'

The Catholic Bishops to the People of Ireland

By the Ecclesiastical Congregation of the Kingdom of Ireland
We, seeing our flocks are misled
By parliamentarian Cromwell of England,
Advise our flocks not to be deluded
By one who would destroy
Religion, life and fortune, if not prevented.
Witness his words to the Governor of Ross:
'Concerning liberty of religion, I meddle not
With any man's conscience, but if by liberty
You mean a liberty to exercise the Mass
I use plain dealing to let you know
This liberty will never come to pass.'
As well as that, Cromwell will sell your land
To greedy bidders out of England.
We cannot, therefore, in our duty to God
And in discharge of the care we bear our flocks
But admonish them not to lose and delude
Themselves with vain hope of conditions
From that merciless enemy. And so, we beseech
The gentry and inhabitants of this island,
Praying that God may save them from evil
And that they serve God in their own land,
To oppose the foe of our religion and King.
As one body, we advance His Majesty's rights
And, in the name of Christ, exhort our flocks
To follow us and our divine light.

Hugo, Joannes, Edmundus, Robertus,
Andreas, Gregorius, Oliverius, Et alii.

An Enlightened Man

'Father Paddy Maguire is an enlightened man.
He forgives the sins of all
Who do the blessed work of the rebel
And tells us the bodies of such men
Are not cold before their souls are in heaven,
Free of purgatorial fire.
Kill, says he, all Protestants in the land,
That's why God planted you here.
Strip every manjack of them then
Take their holy bibles
Lay them on the privy parts of the dead
Open the books at what page you will
And piss your rebels' fill.

If there's worse you can do, fire ahead.'

Larribane Rock

Gilcuff O'Connogher, a bastard son,
Sword at his side, fowling-piece in his hand,
Swore that he knew John Gray was an Englishman
('You have English eyes'), bade him kneel on the ground,
Ordered him out to Larribane Rock,
Stripped him, made him stand in the cold, shivering,
Asked him please to debate the problem
'Shall I hang you now?' John Gray said nothing.
'But this is no dialogue' Gilcuff protested,
'Come let us debate every pro and con,
Else how shall we reach a just solution?'

John Gray said nothing.
                    O'Connogher lifted
His sword, sliced John Gray to the brain
With 'Silent still? Then die by a bastard son.'

Oliver to the Catholic Bishops of Ireland

I wonder not at swirling thoughts and words
At divisions and discontents
Where so anti-christian and sundering a term
As 'Clergy and Laity' is given and received:
A term unknown to any save the anti-christian church
And such as derive themselves from her.
It was your pride gave birth to this expression,
It is for filthy lucre's sake you keep it up.
You make the people believe
They are not as holy as yourselves
So that they, for their penny, may purchase sanctity from you.
You bridle, saddle, ride them at your pleasure.
The obedience of beasts is such
They can't know false from true.
So you dub the people by the name of 'Flocks'.
How dare you call these men your 'Flocks'
Whom you have plunged into rebellion
Till they and all their country are one ruinous heap.
These men you have fleeced, polled, peeled hitherto
And make it your business to do so still.
You cannot feed them! Their hunger is true
While you poison them with false, abominable
Doctrine. You keep the Word of God from them,
You stuff them with senseless Orders and Traditions
Making certain, always, that they cannot choose.
You feed your 'Flocks'
With fear of 'losing their religion'.
Alas, poor creatures! What have they to lose?

Warm

In this moaning place
Where dead and dying
Soldiers are lying
In frozen grass
Barefoot children
Creep from hovels
Cross black ditches
Into freezing fields
Assess all bodies
Halt at the side
Of some dying form
Bare feet meeting
Blood yet living
Are a moment warm.

Dung

'That insatiate rebel, Bryan Boy Magee,
Broke down Sir William Brownlowe's barn wall,
Fired his house which burned fiercely,
Collected the servants, murdered them all.
Next, he turned his eyes on me,
Ordered me, on all fours, to crawl
Before him. I crawled, my hands and knees
Bleeding a little yet glad to be humble..
Not humble enough, though. Bryan Boy Magee,
Bored at the sight of this crawling body,
Stripped me, stabbed me again and again,
Then threw me, amid shouts of rebel glee,
On a dunghill. I lay on the dung, warm, thoughtfully
Bleeding, crawled home, recovered. I'm a new man.'

Conversions

'An Irish priest, Ignatius MacOdeghan,
Captured forty or fifty Protestants,
Persuaded them to abjure their religion
On promise of quarter. These Protestants had sense.

After their abjuration, he asked them if they
Believed that Christ was bodily present in the Host,
That the Pope was the head of the Church,
That the Father, the Son and the Holy Ghost
Were three in one, and one in three?

They did believe, indeed. MacOdeghan,
Happy that they had seen the light
And lest any of the newly-born
Should darken back into heresy,
Cut each converted throat.'

If

If Oliver saw this –
A cold hoarfrosty morning,
Indifferent Earls witnessing through windows
A man, his head grey, his heart breaking,
Somewhat proudly laying that head on the block
As if saying, in better than words, 'There then!'
The Sheriff, with a pitying look,
Offers to let him warm himself again,
Within doors at a fire. But he, 'Nay,
Let us be swift. Soon, my ague will return.
If I be not dead by then, they will say
I tremble for fear.' So, it is done.

If Oliver saw this, I'm sure we'd find
His reflections on the scene would be profound.

Expenses

Survival is a dance among the shapes of death.
Twilight, our killer likes his pint,
Sitting alone, savouring the thought
That once again he knows what he wants.

There will be women, children, a crying shame,
Burning houses, broken walls, blood to be swept
Away by someone with a common name.
There will be those who weep as they have wept

Before. The author of all this
Is ordinary too but knows how to endure
The agony that he dispenses.
He has not changed in a thousand years.
He gives his mind to this, it's what his mind is for,
A costly job, but he'll cover all expenses.

Nails

The black van exploded
Fifty yards from the hotel entrance.
Two men, one black-haired, the other red,
Had parked it there as though for a few moments
While they walked around the corner
Not noticing, it seemed, the children
In single file behind their perky leader,
And certainly not seeing the van
Explode into the children's bodies.
Nails, nine inches long, lodged
In chest, ankle, thigh, buttock, shoulder, face.
The quickly-gathered crowd was outraged and shocked.
Some children were whole, others bits and pieces.
These blasted crucifixions are commonplace.

I Met a Woman

I met a woman in a street somewhere.
She was serious and beautiful. She said
Of the killings, 'Some people are devil-gripped
And many who are not might as well be dead.
If we could only see what is happening
We would never cease to pray.
We would surrender to God's love, knowing
His need for us. There is no other way.'

I said 'Do you pray?'

'I do' she said, 'I let God into me.
I open my heart. He comes.
I pray for the killers, the killed, the ditched women.
I pray for you who are throwing yourselves away.
My heart is stamped with my people's names.'

Volleys

It was a peaceful September night. All that day
People were talking about the apple crop.
At ten o'clock a car load of detectives drove into the place,
Halted in the square, confabbed, looked up
And down the streets, began to question the villagers,
Searched their pockets, smelled their breath, ordered them to wait
Then go straight home. They were to lock their doors
And no matter what happened not to venture out.

Out in the fields the smell of apples sweetened the night air,
There was no thwarting that crop now, summer had kept its promise.
The detectives stood alone in Main Street.
They got into the car, started to drive away.
From the west side of the village ten shots spat out.
It was the second time the volleys were heard that week.

136

Grass

I bought the Barracks where the Tans had been.
It was a shiny-booted man's legs stretched on a table,
Reports on ambush, assassination,
A dirty joke, a no-joking smile,
A wet greatcoat smothering a chair
A button ripped from that same greatcoat
The sound of rifles clicking together
The threat of a midnight fire.

But more than all, it was stone, it was terrible grey stone
That gave orders, judged, told what is forbidden,
Get out, turn round, sign that, shut up, no right to pass.
I sledgehammered it till every stone was down.
I threw every stone into the sea.
I planted grass.

The Voice-of-Us-All

Then the stones cromwelled my head
– O my dandruffed crucified nut –
And I knew I'd never be protected
From this governing rain. I went out
Into the world for the first time in days
Trying to escape, but the first thing I saw
Was a girl with shivering eyes
Singing on a bridge for fear of the law.

The river, polluted as the town,
Made, nevertheless, an effort to flow
Like a cripple determined to live.
I started dancing to avoid the stones,
The girl sang, the law frowned, the river straggled below
And the voice-of-us-all guttered 'Forgive! Forgive!'

Vacancy

Seeking, for once, to better my condition
In life, resolved not to sink under
Those customary waves of squalor
Cromwelling my nightmare head, bruising my skin,
I read like a scholar through my newspaper
Soul and found a vacancy for a hang-
man in the safest jail of our Infant Free State.
At the interview, which I found rather long,
I inquired re the types I'd be expected
To hang. 'Poets' was the reply, 'Poets.
Their bodies in lime, their books off the shelves
Is our aim.' 'That's a bit of a waste' I said
'Don't trouble yourselves with these poor nuts,
Give them enough rope, they'll hang themselves.'

Hero

The manager dressed me up like a queer
I became an artist I made money
An ivory ring dangled from my left ear
My suit of chains rattled merrily
I spoke only of styles of suicide
I hated the non-music I made
Good enough for child-prostitutes though
I called the queen a moron
I stuck a safety-pin through my nose
Dyed my hair pink I insist I'm not primitive
Despite my simian brow
The future is my spit in your face
You can't believe anyone in Government
I'm a hero now.

Resting with Rupert

The King didn't like his six-fingered Queen
So he ordered from France an executioner
Who came to England and cut the head off her
For twenty-three pounds six and eight pence.
The Queen's trunk lay flushing on the scaffold
While her ladies-in-waiting knelt there, weeping.
There was no coffin. A kindly yeoman
Brought an arrow-chest in which the dear thing

Reclined, her head beside her.
Buried in the chapel of St Peter ad Vincula
She reposed for centuries until
Rupert Goodhusband willed to be planted there.
The Queen's bones, stacked in a black casket,
Rest with Rupert; and England is England still.

England

Shat on us for centuries, helped us
When we were down. Pay-packets, parcels, letters home,
Little or no talk of God, Church, Christus Rex,
Very knowledgeable about sex;

Praising our poets for the worst things in their words
Such as flattery and charm,
Forever sending soldiers to bring peace
Watchful and grim

And being always, above all, reasonable,
Graciously accepting every Paddy out of work
Rewarding every man who tries

Like, for example, the Banger Callaghan from Listowel
Who hit for England, his arse through his pants, but came back in a suit
With money and a funny accent and drinks for the boys.

Speech

'Art of Speech?' mused Oliver, 'Into what strange
Regions has it led us, that same sublime
Art. The only man who has a right to speak
Is one whose deeds forever mark his time.

Why listen to others? False speech is most
Accursed, so false it cannot even know
That it is false, as the poor commonplace liar does.
Is man no longer an Incarnate Word

Sent to utter out of him the Godmessage?
Is there no sacredness in the miraculous tongue of man?
Is this head become a wretched cracked pitcher

Jingled to frighten crows and make bees hive?
Come, Buff, let's butcher Rhetoric tonight,
That blasphemous scandalous Misbirth of Nature.'

Mission

Oliver attended a Redemptorist mission
(For men) six winter nights in Caherciveen.
He sat agog, through each night's sermon
Keeping his eyes fixed on the rhetorical man
In the pulpit who roared, for example,
About the evil of french letters in South Kerry.
Now and then, Oliver nodded approval,
Not once did he look bored or weary.

On the last night of the mission, all the faithful
In the Church held burning candles high.
'Do ye renounce the Devil?' asked the passionate man
In the pulpit. 'We do' responded all.
'Louder!' he screamed, 'Do ye renounce the Devil for all eternity?'
'We do, the bastard!' exploded Oliver then.

140

If You Do Not Stop

If you do not stop screaming at me here
In my sleep – I believe I am asleep –
I shall rise up at this post-godly hour
And while millions snore and eleven moons creep
Like a beaten football team down the throats
Of hooting supporters,
                    I shall biff your gob
With my fist until you drop out of your wits.
Should this fail, I'll kick a shin, smash a rib,
Anything to stop you shouting about money.
Join a damned union, organise a protest,
Think of a slogan, chant it, go on strike,
Have meetings, live in the Labour Court,
Make profits, open accounts, do your best
To invest and conquer. I'm sick of your like.

Long After

Long after I have failed
To attend to those humans
Who have every right to my attention
I shall kneel before these hanging dreams
And pray to them
Asking their forgiveness
As once I asked forgiveness of my father
And of God.
And they will fix on me their eyes
Callous-green in their detachment
Laughing like adults at fighting boys
Who must batter each other till one drops
In the shadow of the tall black pole
That lights up at night and dies every morning.

Yes, There, the Clouds

So mauled and stupefied am I at times
I sigh and take old Balder at his word.
The day lights up, I know my parents' names,
The light is something that we might have shared

Had there not been…Ah well, yes, there, the clouds
Again display the shapes that made me once
Create, bad night, my pantheon of gods
Who all agreed that I was such a dunce

I shouldn't be allowed to look at clouds.
But I, your archetypal sneaky weakling,
Angle this dunderhead to spot what I

Can. No gods now. Pigs' bladders bulge with blood,
The stands are packed, the crowds are howling,
I boot these beauties all about the sky.

Brandy

My room went on fire.
I got out, leaned on a hedge, watched it
Spread like a rumour.
A neighbour fumed up to me.

'Suppose it spreads to my place! Eh? What then?'
Another – 'Let it burn. You'll net
A couple of thousand for that!'
Another, a woman, 'Lucky you have no children,

They'd be burned to death by now.'
They milled about me, lurid with complaint and worry.
As I offered my stupid face

Oliver approached and said 'Buffún, you
Look sad. These Irish are a morbid lot, really.
I've seen fires. Come on. There's brandy at my place.'

Portrait

Oliver was having his portrait done.
'If you' he said to the artist, 'are not willing
And able to paint me as the man I am
I won't pay you a single shilling.
I wish to see all my wrinkles and scars,
I am content that my face go forth
Full of sleepless nights, some remorse, long wars,
With valour, policy, authority and worth,
With public care written in all its lines.
Do not belie me with the regular features
And smooth blooming cheeks of some curl-pated minion.'

This portrait hangs in a Lounge Bar in Ballybunion
Admired by aboriginals, tourists, tanned creatures,
With only a few Guinness and spittle stains.
And yet, last night, my grief, a pimply vandal
Hell-bent, as wild-oat hooligans sometimes are
On causing an attention-drawing scandal,
Manned with whiskey scavenged at the bar,
Armed with Daddy's multi-bladed knife
Lifted from that worthy's waistcoat pocket,
Approached the portrait, hating its cold life
And from top to bottom slashed and hacked it.

The Hon. Sec. of the Society
Of the Friends of Cromwell was fit to pee.
'Good Lord!' she anguished; and again 'Good Lord!'

I asked her what the Society planned to do.
'That portrait' she replied 'Is a breakthrough.
Time, skill, expense will see that it's restored.'

Tasty

About two and a half miles up a muddy by-road
Past hedges where summer lovers were wont to rut,
Some ten feet from a sturdy five-bar gate
On a frosty November night,
Dark sparkles jewelling the countryside,
Close to a row of oak-trees
Whose roots, trunks, boughs and leaves
Flourished in the folklore of that parish,

The giant met The Belly. The giant's eyes
Appraised this rural scene with epic relish.

'I'm going to eat you, Belly' smiled the giant.
'Pray don't' The Belly pleaded, 'At least not now;
Ponder somewhat, reflect, be merciful, not hasty.'

For answer, the giant stuffed The Belly in
His gob, chewed the screams, swallowed all
And mumbled 'Not bad. In fact, unusually tasty.'

Hunger

And to what end? A thin saint of a woman,
Well used to the sight of near-skeletons lying
In pavements accustomed to human ruin,
Condemns your dying
Away from what you are to what you
Seem to dream of.
                    Who can sign you back to life?
As you watch your flesh turn black and blue,
Notice your hearing break, your eyes go stiff
And empty, your ulcerated mouth rebel
At water, will you know, even then,
Us, at home, so remote from caring
For you, we stuff our bellies full
At nightfall, sprawl, discuss the sacrifice of one
Who, following directions, died of daring?

An Exchange

Little island developed a stammer, recovered and said
'Big Island, I want to curse you because
You make me feel I'm gone in the head,
Have no respect for God's or man's laws,
Look like an ape, live like a rat,
Think like an ox, have no proper speech,
Walk like a duck, breed like a rabbit.

No wonder I tremble when you approach.

My curse is this: may you get every plague
That heaven and hell can send, may you die
Roaring, may you be known as one who defiled
Every creature living within your range, may you be
Popular, may the ages rain more curses on your head.'

'I'll survive that little outburst' Big Island smiled,

Oliver's Hymn to Hammering

Hammer hammer hammer them down
    Hammer the shrimps among men
Hammer the vermin born to lose
    The cripples who know how to run

Who would be victors? Who would be kings?
    Lords of the land and the sea?
Hammer hammer hammer them down
    And then sing a hymn with me

Sing out a hymn of hammering
    From foot and horse, from tank and jeep
And through this hymn of hammering
    Let such a strong madness sweep
It drowns the coward hearts of all
    Who love to sigh and weep.

Oliver's Prayer

'Lord, though I am a miserable man
I am in covenant with Thee through grace.
If I may, I will come to Thee for Thy people.
Thou hast made me, though unworthy, a mean
Instrument to do them some good, and Thee service.
Many have set too high a value upon me,
Others wish and would be glad of my death.
Lord, however Thou do dispose of me, continue
To do good for Thy people. Forgive their sins,
Do not forsake them, but love and bless them.
May the name of Christ sweeten this English air,
Let me rest in Christ, now and forever.
Pardon such as desire to trample a poor worm
And forgive the folly of this thin prayer.'

The Saddest News

'The saddest news comes today from Piedmont.
The Lord Protector's heart is hit and riven
By the massacre of honest Protestant people
In the valleys of Lucerna and Perosa and St Martin.
The Duke of Savoy sent his preaching friars
To convert these hearts; they would not be converted.
The Duke sent six regiments, three of them Irish,
To kill and maim and banish. All this is not denied.

The Lord Protector is melted in tears, roused into sacred fire.
Let pity be perennial, let England know
The slaughters done by these missioners of hell;
Let a Day of Humiliation be appointed here
Let help be sent to all survivors now
Let blind Milton write harrowingly well.'

Vintage

Jimeen Connor, the butcher, is coming round
The corner of the garage where his cabin
Stands, cosy enough there on sheltered ground.
Passing the spuds and cabbage in his garden
He rams the meathook into Oliver's belly,
Lifts him holus-bolus, hangs him from the iron
Ring. Soon enough, the ground is bloody.
Oliver protests, gurgling. Jimeen is gone
For his hacksaw, he's back, he's cutting
Oliver up, he's catching the blood in a plastic
Bucket, he smiles stretching it towards me:
'I'll have to salt and barrel Olly before eating.
Try this old Puritan wine. Vintage. Knock it back.'

If this is a dream, I dream it scares me
Because the blood of that honest Huntingdon farmer
Turned soldier turned statesman, albeit not wine
As rashly announced by the butcher Connor,
Seemed much the same as yours or mine.
I could have sworn as I stood there watching
It pour into the plastic bucket
I saw and heard the lips murmuring
Religiously, 'Fuck it. Fuck it.'

Next, the butcher – or was it myself? – tipped
The bucket on its side, the blood
Splashed the grass in a red unruly sprawl.
I remember thinking, as the blood escaped
Into the earth, that Oliver did what Oliver did.
So did the butcher. So do I. So do we all.

The Disappearance and Recovery of Oliver

When Cromwell vanished up Mother Ireland's cunt
I stood there, shivering, between her legs
Listening to diminishing screams from that
Gulping haven. First, I threw him a rope
But he could not or would not grasp it.
I tossed him a sniffy Liffey lifebelt
But it fell back and stunned my cranium
So that I lay prone for several seconds.
Rising, though, with the indomitable gusto of my race
I performed a remarkable high jump
Yanking, at the same time, Oliver from his hiding-place.
He was fine, apart from a slight cramp
In his mind and a coating of blood and slime
On his body, which didn't seem to bother him.

The Ship of Flame

The ship of flame defined the Irish sea
Bearing Oliver's corpse home to England
But there were maddened people in that island
Who would not grant him final peace.
So the ship of flame turned back to Ireland
Tried Waterford, Cork, Dublin, Galway
But there were maddened people in that island too
Who refused him burial in their earth.
Then the ship of flame embraced the sea
Went down among the other dead
To find repose among the shells and sand
Among the whispers and the thunders and deceits
Among the weeds and bones and watchful rocks

And there was peace because the sea is blind.

A Will

I, Tom Longley, born in Somersetshire,
Planted in Ireland in 1651,
Now in my right mind and wits, do make
My will as well befits an honest man:

I leave my house, goods and farm to my son
Commonly called Stubborn Jack
Provided only he marries a Protestant
But not that malicious Alice Kendrick
Who called me 'Oliver's whelp'.
My said son Jack shall keep my body
Above ground six days and six nights
After I am dead. Grace Kendrick shall lay me
Out. If she be skilled and willing
Let her be rewarded with five shillings.
My body shall be laid upon
The oak table in the brown room.
Let every corner of the house be clean.
Let fifty mere Irishmen come
To my wake, and let each one
Sink two quarts of the best aquavitae.
Press more on them when they are done.
I pray you, listen well to what they say
Of me as they down that wholesome drink.
If they drink enough they will kill each other.
Don't cease to pour; let every man drink strongly.
When the drink is done, nail up my coffin.
Commit me to the calm earth whence I came.
Witness my hand this day of grace,
                                    Tom Longley.

'Therefore, I Smile'

'Under it all' Oliver said, 'The problem was simple.
How could I make Ireland work?
The Irish hate work, not knowing what it means.
I do. Work exists. It is inevitable and stark,
A dull, fierce necessity. Later ages may consider it
Superfluous but my glimpses of this world were true.
I looked, I saw, I considered, I did what
Was necessary. To live is to work. To be is to do.

Put a man in a field
A soldier fighting a wall
A wife in bed
A whore in a street
A king on a throne

Someone must dig a grave for the dead
And the dead must rot.

Even dead flesh works in the earth
But not the Irish, Buff, not you, not your countrymen.
They will prattle, argue, drink, yarn, but not
Work. Someone had to teach them
Not to idle their lives away.
I taught them to do things my way.
Against their will
I gave them a style.
I tendered them the terrible gift of my name,
Knowing they would make songs about me
Echoing curses soaked in verbal bile
Twisted poems and stories
To make me an excuse for what they
Would fail to do, to be, being themselves.

I am Oliver Cromwell still.

Therefore, I smile.'

Mass-Rock

They were all dead.
My nights were shut of them, my sleep drained,
No more Oliver, Mum, Balder and wife, Ed
Spenser down in Cork fabricating his Queene,

And so, reflecting that not one of these
Souls had, during what is called a lifetime,
Known what I also have failed to know, peace,
I stumbled to a Mass-rock to pray for them.

Picture my distress when I saw before
Me on the rock cats of every hue and breed
Singing in cat-lingo, dancing in a garish pack;

'Shutter the windows! Lock and bar the doors!
Tonight it's certain some of us will bleed!
Attack! Defend! Attack! Defend! Attack!'

A Running Battle

What are they doing now? I imagine Oliver
Buying a Dodge, setting up as a taxi-driver
Shunting three dozen farmers to Listowel Races.
I see Ed Spenser, father of all our graces
In verse, enshrined as a knife-minded auctioneer
Addicted to Woodbines and Kilkenny beer,
Selling Parish Priests' shiny furniture
To fox-eyed housewives and van-driving tinkers.
William of Orange is polishing pianos
In convents and other delicate territories,
His nose purple from sipping turpentine.
Little island is Big, Big Island is little.
I never knew a love that wasn't a running battle
Most of the time. I'm a friend of these ghosts. They're mine.

To Think They All Become Silence

To think they all become silence –
Drogheda cries
Eyes of hanged women
Curses
Burnt houses' trapped people
Churches of excrement
Mockery on the moon's lips
Statesmen's explanatory rant.

To think the silence can erupt
And battles spill again in a quiet street
And the swelling smell of blood guzzle the air
And the earth drink all, trying to forget
But failing and being forced to stand in the dock
Accused, found guilty, sentenced again to suffer, suffer.

A Tail

There was a silent man and a silent woman
Sitting opposite me at table.
'I'd like to talk' I said 'About what I
Believe is wrong.'
                           The man began to smile.
The woman nibbled the house paté.
'There's something we have lost' I continued
'Perhaps not lost. Forgotten. That's the word.'

The man chose ravioli and a bottle of red.
The woman went for veal.
                                'If we put our
Heads together' I said, 'It's possible we may
Remember what it is we have forgotten.'
The man handed me the salt.
                                'You've lost your
Tail' he said, 'Shake this on your arse, twice daily.
Have faith. Persist. Chin up. It may grow again.'

Poisoning the Words

The efficient man was poisoning the words
And the words had the faces of children
Who couldn't see why the man should treat them so.
The words resisted the poison
A while, then painfully gave in.

Malignant white tendrils gripped my tongue
And every stricken word became a stone
In my throat. There is a great wrong
Here, I thought, and what am I doing about it?
I tried to wrench the tendrils from my mouth
But they stuck there.
                              Pray God I'm but dreaming
All this, I pleaded.
                              The children-words were planning
Their escape, silent white seabirds
High over man and tendrils in the October evening.

This

Drag that rat out here into the square.
Does he think he can write a book like this
And get away with it?
Christ Almighty, is there anything he won't say?
How can we protect ourselves against him?

The answer is fire.

Go down on your knees, you scribbling traitor
And ask forgiveness for this
Lewd, disgusting, ugly lie of a thing.
Here's a match, set fire to it yourself,
Then gather the ashes and rub them in your face.
I suppose you think you're telling
Truth. You're a liar and the father of liars.
Come on. Burn this.

The Music Pity Cries For

Who will be there to listen when some singer
Celebrates the pity of all this
God-or-devil-or-man-spawned nightmare
Deepening as the years jeer and sneer at us
I see a boy standing at the gable-end
Of a house from which familiar music
Warms the winter grinding its knives
Against the inside of his skin.

He hardly knows the word,
                                he heard old men
Mutter it once or twice, ·
                                he was born
To make the music pity cries for.
He knows the tricks clouds play with water and stone,
He has time for creatures,
                                his heart won't harden
Wondering what any creature lives and dies for.

The Silent Pits

When all is said and done, not much is done and said.
Moving among the living hordes,
Resurrecting some version of the dead
To flesh them out again with sagging words
Is, given the silent pits, a bit of a game
I learned to play while still a boy
Dreaming of a hole blown in the sky
Through which I'd glimpse the god without a name,
The deft maker of silences, the quiet one
Who asks nothing but absolute attention
And in return puzzles the puzzled mind
Permitting, though, the sight of a cheeky pigeon
Beaking for crumbs among stones in July sun,
Committed to the search, taking what he can find.

Muses

'Today I am a poet' Big Island said
'And let me repeat you do not exist.
Behind me thrive the exemplary dead,
Behind you, scarecrows in a mist
Haggle over halfpennies in the dreepy streets
Of a scuttery town.
My Muse is clean.
Yours is a squat slut in
A cottage at the edge of a village,
Charging sixpence for a fuck.
If times were better, she'd cost more.
She sits there, waiting. Old men trudge
Through the muck towards their sixpenny knock
And a shagged gasp on a kitchen floor.
All lovers
Come and gone, she has a drop of whiskey
Then lies down on her own.
In the morning she goes to a grocer's house,
Scrubs the place from top to bottom.
The grocer emits a randy stink.
The grocer's wife wears a black dress
Suggesting she's a widow before her time.
Your Muse goes down on her knees
To scrub the floors of respectable people.
She's a slave, the way she applies
Herself, but she knows the important gods,
She's fit and willing, a trojan, a genuine girl,
She shifts the filth from decent houses
Then sighs homewards to wait for the lads.'

Two Trains

Three ambulances, braying over the hill,
Cleaner than new blades, all freshly painted,
Shot past, shaking the geranium on the sill,
As if they knew exactly what they wanted.
Although I cannot say that I felt well
I'm very glad they did not stop for me,
Sole witness of some imminent trouble
Embodied in the tall man ten yards away

Staring at me from under the blackest hat
It has been my sad lot to contemplate.
And yet, my contemplation did the trick.
'Get up, you lump' he said, 'Crawl out of that
Stupefying bed. There are two trains to take,
One for the dying, one for the merely sick.'

He, Again

He handed me my shoes.
            'Go now if you
Will' he said, 'To any corner of this
Land. Climb a hill for a different view
Of all that constitutes your catharsis.
Having one's flesh cut up is not without
Advantage. You'll never be afraid again
Of an enormous white bear squinting at
Your fingers, nor will your own skeleton,
So cutely concealed under that immaculate
Skin, bother you for even a moment.
My boy, you'll be able to see in the dark
And from thirty miles spot a woman milking
A young red cow. You'll burn up lies and cant,
Get people back to the sacrament of work.'

'Thanks for the shoes' I said, and started walking.

156

The Traps Are True

I have been walking a long time now, not
Forward as you might expect, but back through
This dirt-road in my head, hedges of thought
Flowering into haws and fuchsia that sprout true
For the time being, anyway. I bang into friends
Whose sons are spitting images of them,
Treasures that the small agonies have found
And nourished even from barren pain and shame

Themselves. I'm bound now for a scarred place
Near the sea. There's a wrecked bridge and big stones.
I love the mud, the wicked thorny-wire
Keeping bulls and cows from the hazardous
Sloblands. Weed greens a greyhound's skull and bones
And an old cormorant plods up the air
Like Bat Weir ambling up his shore meadow
To that corner where he keeps the traps,
Same as his father did decades ago.
The traps are true, Bat says, no creature escapes
'If they're set good'. I believe him. Foxes
May chew their own bones but Bat's not the man
To give them time. I think he'd hear a trap
Snap in his sleep. By the light of pain

He rises in the rewarding night,
Pulls on the trousers and coat, slips out,
Intent under the stars, should there be stars.
Untrapped, the warm dead fox is a fair weight.
Bat turns his back to the sea, the sea-light,
Leaves the cold whispers a grown man ignores.

Home

I respect the foxes, slippery thieves.
I respect the traps, too. I think of hares
Reducing the grass of important graves.
I feel for companionable fears
Driving me to accost some projects that
Consume the best part of my sleeping time
And scornfully outleap my daylight wit.
Yet, though terrorised, I don't give a damn

Because I'm thinking of that dead fox thrown
On the cold flags of Bat's back-kitchen,
In a classical pose, waiting to be skinned,
Lying there beside a bag of onions
Near the yellow wall where Bat's melodeon
Hangs. Out here, I'm listening to a mild wind
And, not for the first time, considering
Sea-light attending to estuary mud.
I could mud myself all over with long
Elegant strokes, then deliberately wade
In for a dip but, catch me, I won't.
Always threatening to do something, that's me.
The sea-light tells me what I can and can't
Achieve at this particular estuary.

I know one thing; sea-light is not the sea
Of which I know so little I can't say
Even now, where it is shallow or deep.

This could be home, God knows, strange territory,
A glimpsed lit strip of sea, shifting, all I
Can ever know of sleeplessness and sleep.

Am

When I consider what all this has made me
I marvel at the catalogue:
I am that prince of liars, Xavier O'Grady,
I am Tom Gorman, dead in the bog,
I am Luke O'Shea in Limerick prison,
I sell subversive papers at a church gate,
Men astound me, I am outside women,
I have fed myself on the bread of hate,
I am an emigrant in whose brain
Ireland bleeds and cannot cease
To bleed till I come home again
To fields that are a parody of peace.
I sing tragic songs, I am madly funny,
I'd sell my country for a fist of money
I am a big family,
I am a safe-hearted puritan
Blaming it all on the Jansenists
Who, like myself, were creatures on the run.
I am a home-made bomb, a smuggled gun.
I like to whine about identity,
I know as little of love as it is possible
To know, I bullshit about being free,
I'm a softie crying at the sound of a bell,
I have a tongue to turn snakespittle to honey,
I smile at the themes of the old poets,
Being lost in myself is the only way
I can animate my foolish wits.

Do I believe myself? I spill
My selves. Believe, me, if you will.

A Soft Amen

The unbelievable dawn is again
Upon me like a chain-letter
Informing me I'm cursed as a man
Unless I copy it out fifty times where
I am right now and send the copies to
Fifty strangers who in turn will each send
Copies to fifty others who in turn...

I

Rise instead,
    Greeting light as a friend
Inviting me out to walk through the grass,
First music of earth, Adam's ears, still in tune,
Filling the world like a soft amen.

This music loves my heart and eyes,
It caresses my blood, kisses my skin
When I bend to pick up a mushroom
Shaped like the white roof of nightmare
Caving in on my sleep.
I know how to laugh, I know how to weep
As morning explodes inside me here
And I'm scattered like, well, I hope

Like Mum and Oliver, Spenser, the giant, William
And all the others striding through me,
Prisoners on parole from history,
Striving to come alive as I think I am,
Finding their food in me, chewing hungrily
First at the edges, then at the core
Of my heart, beating its victim-victor blood
Begetting, forgetting through all my dark and light.

I peel the mushroom, moist flesh of earth and air,
I taste ruined cities of man and God
I hear the makers calling (are the makers mad?)
In the light of day and the light of night.

160

www.ingramcontent.com/pod-product-compliance
Lightning Source LLC
Jackson TN
JSHW020021141224
75386JS00025B/628